Drive and Stroll in

Oxfordshire

Roger Noyce

COUNTRYSIDE BOOKS
NEWBURY BERKSHIRE

First published 2007
© Roger Noyce, 2007

COUNTRYSIDE BOOKS
3 Catherine Road
Newbury, Berkshire

To view our complete range of books,
please visit us at
www.countrysidebooks.co.uk

ISBN 978 1 85306 963 9

Photographs by Margaret and Roger Noyce

Cover picture of the River Thames at Iffley
supplied by Bill Meadow

Designed by Peter Davies, Nautilus Design
Produced through MRM Associated Ltd., Reading
Printed by Borcombe SP Ltd., Romsey

Contents

Contents

PUBLISHER'S NOTE

We hope that you obtain considerable enjoyment from this book; great care has been taken in its preparation. Although at the time of publication all routes followed public rights of way or permitted paths, diversion orders can be made and permissions withdrawn.

We cannot, of course, be held responsible for such diversion orders and any inaccuracies in the text which result from these or any other changes to the routes nor any damage which might result from walkers trespassing on private property. We are anxious, though, that all details covering the walks are kept up to date and would therefore welcome information from readers which would be relevant to future editions.

The simple sketch maps that accompany the walks in this book are based on notes made by the author whilst checking out the routes on the ground. They are designed to show you how to reach the start, to point out the main features of the overall circuit and they contain a progression of numbers that relate to the paragraphs of the text.

However, for the benefit of a proper map, we do recommend that you purchase the relevant Ordnance Survey sheet covering your walk. The Ordnance Survey maps are widely available, especially through booksellers and local newsagents.

Introduction

The sparkle of a country river meandering through a scenic valley, colourful narrow boats passing under an historic, ornate canal bridge, and peaceful reflections on beautiful lakes and reservoirs. These are just some of the delights that you can enjoy in abundance in Oxfordshire. There are meandering hills that invite you to share their stunning views, there are walks in attractive woodland through a carpet of bluebells in spring and, in summer, you can stroll through fields of golden wheat or vivid yellow rape. Red kites flying high over tree-covered hilltops add romance to some of the walks and there are so many wonderful places to visit.

These strolls offer you the opportunity to venture into some of Oxfordshire's most attractive villages, where picture-postcard pubs form the base for many of the walks. Stroll through the attractive Cotswold villages of Great Tew and Wroxton, where thatched cottages line the streets. Or walk along public footpaths through the Great Park at Woodstock, where you can enjoy superb views of Blenheim Palace. Some of the circuits take you along parts of the famous Ridgeway, which offers exceptionally fine scenery in the Chilterns Area of Outstanding Natural Beauty. The Oxford Canal was built in the late 18th century to link the River Thames with Midlands industry and on several of the walks you can saunter along its fine towpath.

The 20 strolls chosen for this book seek to explore Oxfordshire's feast of history, its amazing ancient buildings, its gentle rolling countryside, its fine hills and its warm welcome. They are generally undemanding and should be suitable for families with children who want to explore our wonderful countryside. Mileages given are approximate, with the strolls varying in length from 3 to 6 miles. Except for the Country Parks, you will need good strong footwear, as some of the walks could be muddy in wet weather, when a waterproof may also be required – a daysack is useful for carrying drinks, snacks, and spare clothing. Occasionally I have used pay and display car parks where the charges are normally low and I'm sure you will feel the amenities they offer will justify the modest expense.

All of the routes incorporate public rights of way, where there is an onus upon every walker to always follow the Country Code, to look after our precious countryside and to protect the environment for future generations. Remember to leave only footprints and to take away only photographs and memories.

Although a sketch map is provided for each walk I recommend you to acquire the relevant Ordnance Survey Explorer maps when walking these routes – details of these are included with each walk.

I invite you to stroll along the lovely footpaths in the beautiful county of Oxfordshire.

Happy walking.

Roger Noyce

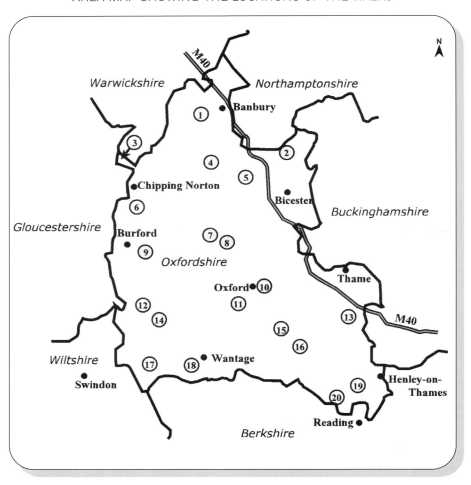

1

Wroxton and North Newington

The village pond in Wroxton

The Walk 3 miles
Terrain Initially undulating and then along good footpaths and farm tracks.
Map OS Explorer 191 Banbury, Bicester and Chipping Norton
(GR 414417)

How to get there

Wroxton is about 3 miles west of Banbury on the A422 (Stratford-upon-Avon) road. Go left into the village, passing the church, to arrive near to the North Arms pub and the village pond. **Parking:** Park, with consideration, near to the pond in Wroxton.

Drive and Stroll

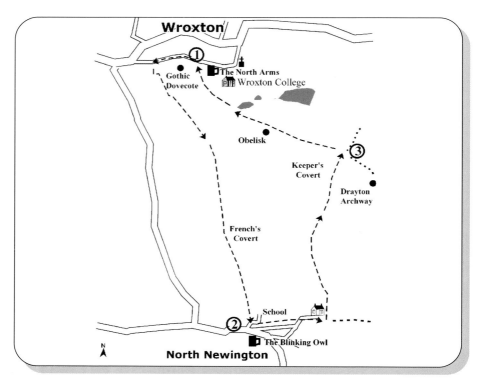

Introduction

This lovely stroll starts by the pond in historic Wroxton, probably the most picturesque village in Oxfordshire. There is even a thatched duck house on a little island in the middle of the pond. Wroxton should perhaps be called the 'Sundial Capital of Oxfordshire' – see if you can find them all. At the crossroads just to the west of the village is a very fine sundial with four faces and carved stone hands pointing the way to London, Banbury and other places. There is a sundial on the south wall of the church, and nearby a small ceramic sundial in the wall of the Old Workshop. The North Arms has one and there is another by the duck pond. A few doors up the street is Sundial Farmhouse, which has had a dial for hundreds of years although the present one is modern and unfortunately does not tell the right time! After exploring this pretty village the walk takes you through delightful Cotswold countryside, with fine views, to the village of North Newington and returns to pass near two of the 'eyecatchers' built to enhance the outlook from Wroxton Abbey – the Drayton Archway and the Gothic Dovecote.

The North Arms

This beautiful 17th-century inn is situated outside the entrance to Wroxton Abbey and is a treat to behold. It displays a deer on its thatched roof, has a fine old sundial with the motto *Sic transit gloria mundi* (Thus passes the glory of the world) and a delightful garden. Originally the building was a row of cottages, converted to a public house in 1850. You will be made very welcome and can enjoy a fine lunch, selecting from a menu which offers good food from snacks, soups and rolls to T-bone steaks. To eat out in the lovely garden on a sunny day is rather special. Telephone: 01295 730318.

THE WALK

From the village pond proceed up **Wroxton's** main street.

Wroxton offers the quintessential English village scene so take your time to admire its thatched cottages, village pond (with ducks) and thatched pub. Behind the walls is Wroxton Abbey, set amid beautiful lawns, gardens and woodland. To the writer Henry James, this remarkable Jacobean manor house was part of the essence of England. It is now known as Wroxton College and is occupied by the Fairleigh Dickinson University.

In about 275 yards, go left and ascend a path to the left of **Wroxton primary school**. Proceed over a couple of stiles, along the left-hand edge of a field and past barns to a farm gate, where you can enjoy the view. Follow the clear waymarker signs and ascend the other side of the valley, passing to the right of woodland called **French's Covert**.

Continue ahead over several fields and stiles, crossing more attractive hilly pastureland. All too soon you will be descending towards the village of **North Newington** and arrive at a lane via another stile.

Turn left and stroll along the road. At the road bend, proceed ahead along a footpath set at the bottom of the playing area of **Bishop Carpenter primary school**, then continue along the back of the houses to arrive in **School Lane**. Cross the lane and stroll down the footpath in the field to the right of a cottage. Exit the field via the stile and now turn sharp left onto a clear signed footpath going northwards through a delightful valley. Cross over a stream, pass to the right of **Keeper's Covert** and arrive at a junction of footpaths with an impressive obelisk to your left. Up the hill to the right you will see an 'eyecatcher' – the **Drayton Archway**.

The Drayton Archway was designed by Sanderson Miller (1717–1780), a

Drive and Stroll

The North Arms pub has a delightful garden

leading exponent of Gothic Revival
architecture and a garden designer,
and is sited so as to be seen from the
gardens of Wroxton Abbey.

  (3)

Turn left and ascend the hill past the
obelisk, erected in 1739 to
commemorate the visit of Frederick,
Prince of Wales. Proceed over the
stile near to the obelisk, pausing to
enjoy the view over **Wroxton College**
and its fine gardens. Continue over
the stiles to the left of the gardens
(there is an attractive pool) and go
through the farm gate, ascending
through a hand-gate into pastureland

to the **Gothic Dovecote**.

*The Gothic Dovecote was also built
by Sanderson Miller in 1745, on the
highest ground near to the abbey. It
has loop windows, battlements and a
fine banner-type weathervane.
Wroxton Abbey was the home of Lord
North, Prime Minister 1770–1782,
who has gone down in history as the
man who lost the American colonies
in the War of Independence.*

From the gate, bear right along the
well-used path to a kissing-gate and
descend by the edge of the **College**
gardens to return to the village pond.

PLACES OF INTEREST NEARBY

Wroxton Abbey is not open to the public, but the gardens are, every day
from dawn to dusk. Website: www.gardenvisit.com
Banbury, the historic town of nursery-rhyme fame, is just 3 miles to the east.
Its waterside museum is open daily and tells the story of the town, with
'hands on' displays. Telephone: 01295 259855.

2 Cottisford and Tusmore Park

A delightful scene in Cottisford

The Walk 3½ miles
Terrain An easy walk, mainly on farm tracks.
Map OS Explorer 191 Banbury, Bicester and Chipping Norton
(GR 587310)

How to get there

From the A4421 about 3 miles north of Bicester, turn left and follow the signs into Fringford, and then on to Hethe. Now continue along country lanes into Cottisford. **Parking:** Go left at the crossroads and park with consideration by the roadside near to St Mary's church.

11

Drive and Stroll

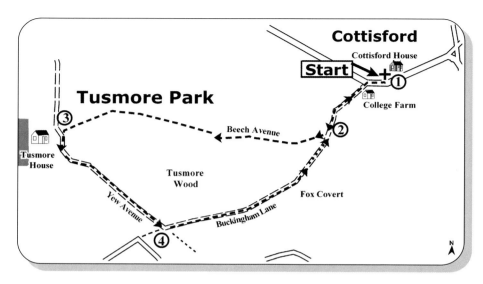

Introduction

There can be few more pleasant walks than this exploration of the area around historic Cottisford, in the heart of Flora Thompson country. In 1900 the village comprised just 30 cottages and Flora brought the community here vividly to life in her book *Lark Rise to Candleford*. She recorded that the standing joke about the tiny village was that when a traveller asked the way to Cottisford, he was told that he had just walked right through it. There is a plaque to her memory in the church, where you can also obtain interesting booklets about the area. This easy walk takes you through the village and on to superb Tusmore Park, passing close to its house, before returning along good tracks back into Cottisford.

The Peyton Arms

This country pub, situated at Stoke Lyne, approximately five miles south-west of Cottisford is a real treat. Built in warm Cotswold stone and dating back to the 1800s, it was originally called the Royal George, but was renamed in the 1850s in honour of Sir Henry Peyton, who was then Lord of the Manor. It is a popular place with the locals who like to swap stories and exchange gossip – the local talking shop where spirits and glasses are lifted. This is a traditional pub where walkers are made welcome and home-cooked pub food and sandwiches are very popular. Hook Norton real ales are drawn straight from the cask. You may eat in the small snug, the lounge or the large garden, which you may have to share with geese and rabbits – or even two pygmy goats on leads brought by one local. The bar is open Monday to Friday from noon to 2.30 pm and 6 pm to 11.30 pm; from noon to 11 pm on Saturday (10.30 pm on Sunday). Telephone: 01869 345285. **Email:** info@ peytonarms.com

Just three miles south of Cottisford, at Fringford, is the Butchers Arms which is open every day of the week. Telephone: 01869 277363.

THE WALK

From the church of **St Mary the Virgin**, head right and stroll up through the village of **Cottisford**.

This tiny village was founded in Saxon times and, in 1066 after the Battle of Hastings, William the Conqueror gave the manor to the Norman baron Hugh de Grantmesnil as a reward for his valiant services. Today it is renowned for its connection with Flora Thompson, who was born Flora Jane Thimms in 1876 at Watford Tunnel Cottage in the neighbouring hamlet of Juniper and who spent most of her childhood at the End House, since renamed 'Larkrise Cottage'. She went to school in Cottisford.

In about 150 yards, turn left along a clear farm track, passing by the building conversions of **College Farm**. Continue down the wide track for about 500 yards.

Now turn right (west) and continue along a pleasant green track set to

the left of the field hedge. This easy walking will soon bring you through a beautiful avenue of beech trees on the approach to **Tusmore Park**. Bear right and then left to continue towards the main park. Walk a stone track set to the left of more lovely beeches to arrive in the park, where the superb trees can be enjoyed in their full splendour. The now green track arcs left towards the impressive building of **Tusmore House** and you will arrive on the driveway to this fine mansion which is privately owned.

In medieval times Tusmore was a village but its population was wiped out by the Black Death in about 1385. Sir Roger de Cottisford built the first Tusmore House and set it in a vast area of beautiful parkland. The present Tusmore House was built in the 20th century and is the fifth house to be built on the site.

Bear left (southwards) along the main driveway, passing to the left of the house. Continue along the driveway/track, along **Lime Avenue** which bears slightly left to become **Yew Avenue**.

Drive and Stroll

St Mary the Virgin church in Cottisford

 (4)

At a clear junction of tracks, bear left onto **Buckingham Lane**, now walking in a north-easterly direction. This is an excellent track with the superb trees of **Tusmore Wood** to the left. Soon you pass through a narrow strip of woodland and leave **Tusmore Wood** to cross pastureland, still maintaining your north-easterly direction. The track takes you to the left of **Fox Covert** and veers more northwards until you meet up with the wide track again. Retrace your steps along this track back into the village of **Cottisford**.

PLACES OF INTEREST NEARBY

Bicester Village Retail Park is 8 miles to the south, an international outlet shopping centre that offers a day out for the family, with over 60 designer and famous brand names represented. Website: www.bicestervillage.com

3 Adlestrop and Chastleton House

On the track to Peasewell Wood

The Walk 3 miles
Terrain Good footpaths, country lanes and farm tracks.
Map OS Outdoor Leisure 45 The Cotswolds (GR 242273)

How to get there

From the A44, 3 miles west of Chipping Norton, turn left onto the A436. After about 2 miles, turn right and follow the signs into Adlestrop. **Parking:** In the village car park at Adlestrop, next to the village hall (donations sought).

Drive and Stroll

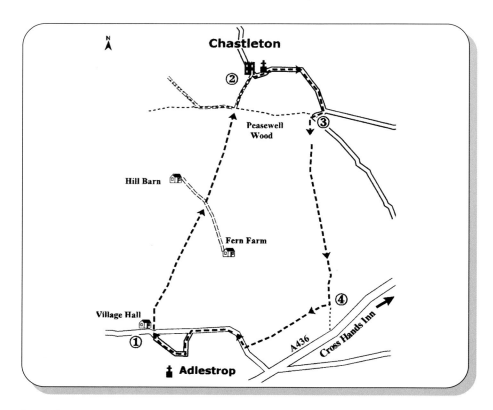

Introduction

Enjoy this lovely walk in the Cotswolds from the beautiful village of Adlestrop, made famous in the poem by Edward Thomas: 'Yes. I remember Adlestrop –'. There are plenty of good views along the route, over the surrounding hills and the Evenlode valley, before you reach Chastleton House, a gem of a 17th-century house in the care of the National Trust. If you want to look round Chastleton, admission is by timed ticket and it is best to telephone the day beforehand to book, as visitor numbers are strictly limited – otherwise it is 'first come first served' (telephone: 01608 674355). A delightful stretch of walking brings you back into Adlestrop to complete a fascinating day out.

The Cross Hands Inn

Situated at the junction of the A44 and A436, the Cross Hands Inn has been a popular resting place for travellers since the 16th century and remains a favourite watering hole for local ramblers. It is believed to be the highest public house in Oxfordshire and has fine views over the surrounding countryside. During the Second World War, Winston Churchill visited here when he reviewed the Royal Durham Regiment stationed at nearby Adlestrop. You will get a warm welcome and an excellent meal at a reasonable cost. The extensive menu includes chef's specials, and the Cross Hands Chicken is a favourite with many – chicken breast topped with bacon in a barbecue sauce served with vegetables and new potatoes. Telephone: 01608 643106. Website: www.crosshandsinn. co.uk

THE WALK

Leave the car park in **Adlestrop** by going left and turning immediately left again up a signed footpath by the side of the village hall. This wide track passes to the right of a horse-riding area and you will go over a stile at the end of the meadow. Continue along the signed path, aiming for a stile/gate in the far corner of the next field. In a few yards, turn left over a further stile, then go right, walking by the right-hand hedge of the next field to reach another stile in its far right-hand corner – you will see the ruins of **Hill Barn** up the hill to your left. Proceed diagonally and ascend the next field to a stile set in the trees in the top left-hand corner. Pause here to enjoy a fine retrospective view of **Broadwell** and the hills surrounding the **Evenlode valley**.

Continue up the track through the trees and walk a clear path over a cultivated field, strolling over the brow of the hill – there is a pleasant view of the surrounding hills. Soon you will

reach the left-hand corner of **Peasewell Wood**. At the field end, go through a metal gate with a blue waymark and proceed down an avenue of trees to arrive on the road in the village of **Chastleton**.

Turn right and stroll past the front of beautiful **Chastleton House**, with 12th-century **St Mary's church** by its side. Note the superb dovecote in the field opposite, to the right.

Chastleton House is a fine Jacobean mansion, built in 1603 by a local wool merchant who had purchased the site from Robert Catesby, of Gunpowder Plot fame. The building hides a secret room within its massive walls, which hid a fugitive from the battle of Worcester during the Civil War.

Continue along the road and pass the National Trust car park. The road bends right and you continue to the next road corner. Here, turn right towards the end of **Peasewell Wood**.

Drive and Stroll

Charming cottages in Adlestrop

 (3)

Do not enter the woodland but bear left and proceed down a good grass track into open countryside. This is a lovely track with fine views all around and particularly to the right. After just over half a mile of delightful walking you reach the edge of woodland and then, in a further 200 yards, a junction of footpaths.

 (4)

Here, turn right and proceed along an avenue of trees to reach a road. Turn right and stroll down the quiet country road towards the village of

Adlestrop. In about 500 yards turn left into **Schooler's Lane** and follow the lane round into the main street of the village.

If you can spare the time, perhaps continue up the lane to visit the fine village church.

Stroll down the main street and take your time to enjoy the beautiful period cottages lining the road. At the bottom you will pass a fascinating station sign that decorates the bus stop on the corner near the village hall, from where it is a short step back to your car.

PLACES OF INTEREST NEARBY

The **Rollright Stones** are situated high on an exposed ridge near Long Compton. They are best reached by taking the A436 road and crossing the A44 onto a minor road that leads to Long Compton. The most important stone circle in England after Stonehenge and Avebury, the stones are believed to be about 3,500 years old.

4 Great Tew

The 'Cat Walk' in Great Tew

The Walk 4½ miles
Terrain One short ascent, then mostly on good footpaths and tracks
Map OS Explorer 191 Banbury, Bicester and Chipping Norton
(GR 395293)

How to get there

Great Tew is 6 miles north-east of Chipping Norton. From the A361 Banbury road, turn right onto the B4022 which leads into the village. **Parking:** In the free car park at the entrance to Great Tew.

Drive and Stroll

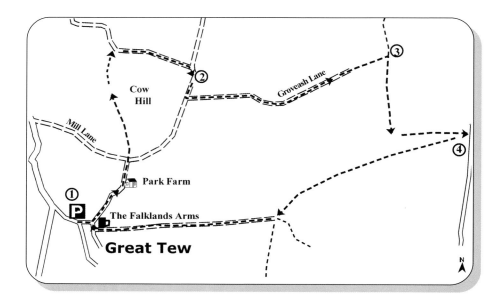

Introduction

A fine hill walk in North Oxfordshire starting from the peaceful village of Great Tew, where honey-coloured stone cottages surround the lovely village green. Constructed by 19th-century landscape gardener, John Loudon, as part of an extensive park overlooking the Worton Valley, Great Tew is a picture-postcard Cotswold village consisting of delightful cottages with thatched and gabled roofs, mullioned windows and charming flower beds, set amid green meadows and fruit orchards which run down to a little brook. From here the route takes you over Cow Hill for a fine retrospective view over the village. Then a good farm track leads you through superb scenery. There are pleasing views all around and, as you stroll by the side of Great Tew Park, you may see lapwings nesting in the fields. You will be greeted by the sight of the Falkland Arms, a beautiful thatched inn, and those stunning thatched cottages on your return to Great Tew. A super walk with much to enjoy.

The Falkland Arms

This award-winning Cotswold inn is a regular haunt of local walkers and you are guaranteed a warm welcome. It dates back to the 16th century and was originally called the Horse and Groom. Set at the end of a row of thatched properties, it is a treat to visit and you can sit out in the front garden and enjoy the unique atmosphere of the Cotswolds. In winter, you can sit by the inglenook fireplace and admire a fantastic collection of mugs and jugs that hang from the ceiling and the selection of clay pipes and snuff on sale. The inn provides delicious, home-made food sourced from locally produced ingredients between 12 noon and 2 pm and from 7 pm to 8 pm every day of the week. It is a traditional country bar menu, with hand-raised pork pies and beef and ale pie being two of the favourites with locals. Perhaps local pork and herb sausages with scrumptious mash and cider gravy will be your preference. You can enjoy 'good value for money' food in an intimate dining room or you may wish to eat out on the front patio or in the attractive rear garden. You will not be disappointed. Telephone: 01608 683653. Website: www.falklandarms.org.uk

THE WALK

(1)

From the village car park, turn left to arrive in the middle of the village and then go left again at the fine thatched post office. Continue by strolling along **Brook Road**, taking time to admire the many thatched cottages. After passing by **Bee Bole Cottage** the road bends left and descends past **Lower Park Farm**.

At the bottom leave the road/track and proceed ahead over a stile to ascend **Cow Hill** – a fairly steep climb but you are rewarded with an excellent view over **Great Tew**. Continue ahead over the stile by the farm gate and now descend the other side of **Cow Hill**. After going over a further stile you will arrive on a lane. Go right along this lane (little more than a farm track) and in about 600 yards you will arrive back on the main track.

(2)

Now go right and then in about 50 yards turn left along a farm track known as **Groveash Lane**. Follow this for the next 1½ miles.

(3)

At the junction of paths, turn right along a footpath over cultivated land. Cross the footbridge over the stream and continue to a gap in the next field hedge. Here, turn left through the farm gate and stroll up towards a lane.

(4)

Do not go onto the lane but turn back on yourself and walk along the footpath that runs nearly parallel with the path you have just walked, aiming for a stile set about 100 yards to the left of the field gate you came through. Go over this stile and continue in a generally south-westerly direction over lovely open fields for about 1¼ miles. At the field corner, bear right and walk the

Drive and Stroll

clear headland footpath set to the right of the stone wall to **Great Tew Park**.

Many of the fine trees in Great Tew Park are part of the planting done by the landscape gardener, John Loudon, who was manager of the estate in the early 19th century. It is a popular location for film and television companies and the BBC used it as a setting for some of the scenes from its 1999 adaptation of David Copperfield.

Proceed along this good path/track into the village of **Great Tew**. You will arrive by the side of the **Falkland Arms** inn. Turn right and then go left to return to the car park.

PLACES OF INTEREST NEARBY

Hook Norton Brewery is 4 miles north-west in the village of Hook Norton and has a visitor centre with guided tours. Telephone: 01295 730384.
Broughton Castle, the ancestral home of the Saye family, is 8 miles to the north in a romantic setting in the village of Broughton. Telephone: 01295 276070. Website: www.broughtoncastle.com.

5 | Lower Heyford

The towpath of the Oxford Canal at Lower Heyford

The Walk 5 miles
Terrain An easy level walk along mainly good footpaths, country lanes and the canal towpath.
Map OS Explorer 191 Banbury, Bicester and Chipping Norton
(GR 486247)

How to get there

Lower Heyford is 7 miles west of Bicester on the B4030. **Parking:** There is limited roadside parking in Market Square or, with consideration, along the side of Freehold Road.

Drive and Stroll

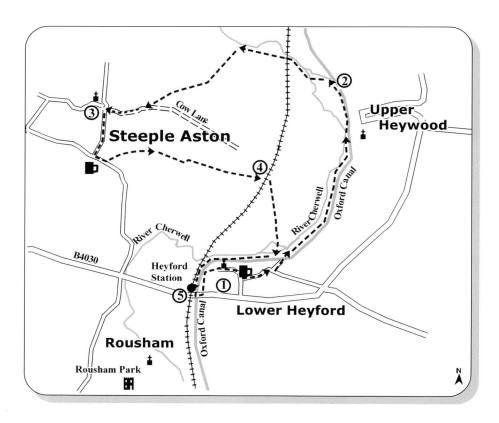

Introduction

This pleasing walk starts in the attractive village of Lower Heyford which, until the 13th century, was known simply as Heyford. You walk parallel with the river along the towpath of the Oxford Canal, which was opened in 1790 to transport coal to the Midlands, and then stroll across lovely countryside into Steeple Aston – a delightful village of stone houses and cottages which was established as a market town of some 200 souls at the time of the Domesday Book. There is an alabaster effigy of its most famous 18th-century resident, Sir Francis Page – the Hanging Judge – in the parish church. The route continues by passing near to the 'eyecatcher' which was built as a landscape feature for nearby Rousham House. You then return to the Oxford Canal, walking its towpath once again to pass a colourful wharf and some fine stone houses.

The Bell Inn

The 18th-century Bell Inn was originally a Wesleyan chapel and was then converted into two cottages before it became the attractive pub it is today. Being situated near to the Oxford Canal, many narrowboat owners are regular customers and the inn offers a good mixture of foods from baguettes to lasagne and steak. There is something to suit every palette on the menu board and it is a treat to eat out and sup a pint of best real ale in the large garden. Telephone: 01869 347176.

THE WALK

(1)

From **Market Square** head left along **Freehold Street** into the village, where a number of thatched buildings catch the eye and you pass the **Old Bakery** and the **Old Bakehouse**. Bear left down **Mill Lane**. At the **Oxford Canal** turn right along the towpath, which runs parallel with the **River Cherwell**. Proceed past **Allen's Lock** to reach **Bridge 203**.

 (2)

Turn left to leave the towpath and enter a large field. Bear right across the concrete bridge over a stream. Then turn right again, walking parallel with the stream, and go through the tunnel beneath the railway line. From the tunnel walk along the narrow footpath into the next field to reach a waymarked bridge at the edge of woodland. Cross over this bridge and proceed through a narrow stretch of trees into a cultivated field. At the top of the field pass through the wide hedgerow into the next field, where

you walk to the right of woodland – follow the field-edge path and go through the farm gate onto a farm track (called **Cow Lane**). Turn right along **Cow Lane**, gently ascending towards **Steeple Aston** village. You will arrive in the village at a T-junction near to the impressive church.

Note the preschool at the road corner. This was founded as a school in 1640 by Dr Samuel Ratcliffe. He was also responsible for the two almshouses nearby, which are administered by the Radcliffe Trust. A technical school was part of the group of buildings but this has since been converted to become the village hall. From the road you can see the inscription on the school building: 'Feed my Lambs'.

 (3)

Turn left down **Paines Hill**, taking time to enjoy the lovely village scene. All too soon you will reach the road near to the **White Lion** pub. Go left along this quiet road for about 50 yards, then bear left and head down a lane called **The Dickridge**. After passing some attractive cottages you

Drive and Stroll

The 'eyecatcher' in the grounds of Rousham House

arrive on a concrete farm lane by a fingerpost which says 'Lower Heyford 2'. Continue through two kissing-gates and a hand-gate to reach a small area of woodland where, to your left, you will see the 'eyecatcher' for **Rousham House**. Continue over a stile, then walk through a narrow plantation of trees. A further stile leads back into pastureland and you descend to reach and go across the bridge over the mainline railway.

Bear right immediately after crossing the bridge and diagonally cross pastureland in a generally southerly direction. Go over the stile at the field corner and proceed along the tree-lined path by the **River Cherwell**. Cross over the river bridge onto the towpath of the **Oxford Canal** and head right, walking in a westerly direction. You will find a number of colourful narrow boats moored on the canal. In about 200 yards you can take a shortcut over a canal bridge to arrive back in the centre of **Lower Heyford** village near to the **Bell Inn**. The full route continues along the towpath, which arcs left, and you pass by the attractive **Lower Heyford Wharf** to reach the main B4030 near to **Heyford station**.

(5)

Go left over the stone bridge set immediately before the main road and ascend past the entrance to **Lower Heyford Wharf**. In 20 yards, turn left through a kissing-gate and proceed along a good footpath past the recreation area. You will pass to the right of the wharf and just before you reach the canal, bear right, proceed through a hand-gate and walk along the short hedged path to arrive on the road near to **St Mary's church**. Continue along the road and soon you will arrive in the centre of the village by the **Bell Inn**.

PLACES OF INTEREST NEARBY

Rousham Park is well worth a visit. Designed in the 18th century by William Kent, who has been dubbed the 'father of the landscape garden', it has changed remarkably little since that time. Telephone: 01869 347110; www.rousham.org

Drive and Stroll

6 Foxholes Nature Reserve

Foxholes in springtime

The Walk 3 miles
Terrain An easy walk on good paths, farm tracks and country lanes.
Map OS Outdoor Leisure 45 The Cotswolds (GR 258208)

How to get there

Foxholes Nature Reserve is 5½ miles south-west of Chipping Norton. From the A424 take the road to Bruern Abbey. About ¼ mile past the turn to Milton under Wychwood, take the rough track to the left, following the edge of the woodland for ½ mile. **Parking:** Foxholes Nature Reserve car park (free).

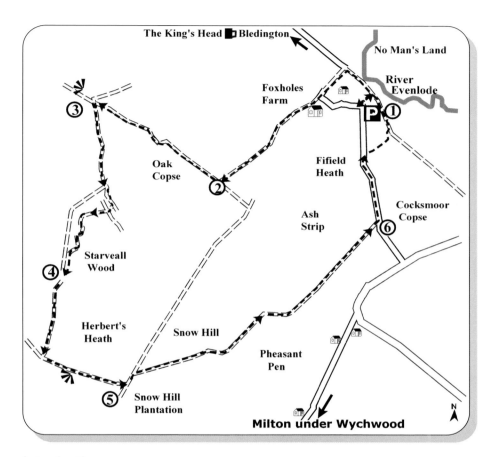

Introduction

This delightful stroll takes you around Foxholes, one of the most beautiful nature reserves in Oxfordshire, for a special wildlife treat. Once part of the ancient Wychwood Forest, Foxholes in the spring is a veritable treasure because the ground is covered with a carpet of beautiful bluebells, primroses, red campion, violets and orchids. The cuckoo call will seem to follow you around the reserve and you should look out for the treecreeper and the nuthatch. In the summer, foxgloves, devil's bit scabious and spotted orchids can be found and you are likely to see the sparrowhawk, kingfishers and the little owl. White admiral, comma, speckled wood and ringlet butterflies are in profusion. The woodland is alive with birds chirruping away. This is the countryside at its very best.

Drive and Stroll

The King's Head Inn

This lovely 16th-century pub at Bledington, approximately 2¾ miles north-west of Foxholes, was once a cider house. The first man of repute to 'sign the visitors book' was Prince Rupert of the Rhine, who lodged here prior to the Battle of Stow in 1646, during the Civil War. Being situated in a Royalist area, it is likely that the pub got its name after the restoration of the monarchy in 1660. The inn is situated near to a stream in the dreamy village of Bledington – one of the most beautiful villages in the Cotswolds, having more than once won the Bledisloe Cup for the Best Kept Village Award. You will be made very welcome at the King's Head, where delicious food is served every day. Who could resist the steak and Hook Norton stew topped with mash and puff pastry, or perhaps you only have time for a toasted panini sandwich? Telephone: 01608 658365.

THE WALK

Exit the car park onto the track and turn right, then right again down a footpath by the side of the car park to reach a bridlepath. Turn left along the bridlepath and you will see through the woodland edge towards the **Evenlode river**. In about 300 yards, turn left up a farm driveway, passing to the right of **Foxholes Farm** to a bridlegate. Go through this and stroll up through pastureland to a second bridlegate into the lovely woodland of **Chancellor's Oaks**. Proceed through the trees, gently ascending the track for about ½ mile to reach a junction of paths.

Turn right and continue along the very clear route through the woodland, now in **Oak Copse**. Stroll up the main path through the trees, following blue bridleway markers, and in about 650 yards you will reach another junction of paths, now with yellow waymarkers. The route of the blue waymarker brings you into open farmland for a pleasing viewpoint over the neighbouring countryside.

Return to the junction and the yellow waymarkers. Now bear right along the footpath that heads generally southwards near to the edge of the copse. In about 400 yards (at the corner of the woodland) you will reach a rail and a junction of paths. Turn right and proceed along the path that appears to move away from the wood edge. In just over 100 yards the path bends left, but here you turn right along a main forest track. This lovely track zigzags through the trees and you will arrive near the edge of the woodland. Turn left onto a well-walked footpath that hugs the edge of **Starveall Wood**, going southwards once again.

On the route

 ④

Walk this path to the end of **Herbert's Heath** – as the path progresses by the wood edge it is partly to the right of a rather tired-looking barbed wire fence and you will notice that you have arrived in an area of conifer trees. At the end of the wood exit the trees and turn left onto a wide grass bridlepath with open views to your right. Stroll along this good grass track, passing by the small plantation of young conifers and some attractive gorse bushes. At the field end you will meet a track coming in from the right.

 ⑤

Turn left into the trees and in 75 yards you will reach a junction of tracks. Do not continue along the track going into the trees. The bridlepath to the right is the **D'Arcy Dalton Way**, but for now you follow the direction of the **Claude du Val** route, which takes you outside the trees following the track across the field to reach the corner, where you now join the **D'Arcy Dalton Way**. At the field end, bear right and then turn left through a farm gate with a **D'Arcy Dalton** waymarker on the post. Ascend the good stone farm

31

Drive and Stroll

track past a row of oak and beech trees. At the rise the track bends right and then left to go over a cattle grid (or through the bridlegate), and then continues to a T-junction of farm tracks. Turn right and then go immediately left to descend a wide grass track on the right of the hedge with **Home Farm Cottages** to your right.

 6

At the bottom of the field you reach the road. Turn left along the rather pitted lane – you may meet horses on exercise. In about 350 yards go right over a stile and cross a buttercup field to a second stile to enter **Cocksmoor Copse**. Turn left along the bridlepath and stroll along this until you reach a junction of paths. Turn left to return to the car park.

PLACES OF INTEREST NEARBY

Burford, 5 miles to the south, is a beautiful town that is generally regarded as the 'Gateway to the Cotswolds'. There are many attractive buildings, including the fine church by the River Windrush. Telephone: 01993 823558; email: burfordvic@westoxon.gov.uk

Or, 8 miles to the west, there is **Bourton-on-the-Water**, a 'chocolate box' village known as the 'Venice of the Cotswolds'. Telephone: 01451 820211; email: bourtonvic@cotswold.gov.uk

7 | Woodstock and Blenheim Park

Looking over Queen Pool to Blenheim Palace

The Walk 5½ miles
Terrain Easy walking along good footpaths
Map OS Explorer 180 Oxford, Witney and Woodstock (GR 446168)

How to get there

Woodstock is 7½ miles north-west of Oxford on the A44. Hensington Road is to the right just after you pass the entrance gates to Blenheim Palace, as you enter the village. **Parking:** In Hensington Road pay and display car park.

Drive and Stroll

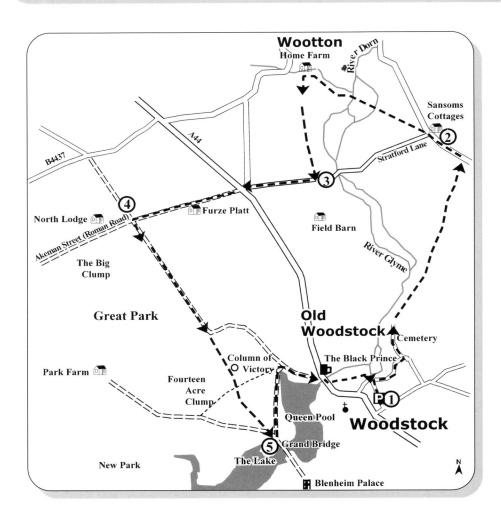

Introduction

Open countryside and views over the valley of the rivers Dorn and Glyme make a wonderful start to this walk, which then brings you back through Blenheim Park for a short stroll in the famous gardens. Here you can enjoy a superb view of Blenheim Palace before returning to delightful Woodstock. Spare time to stroll around this thriving town. It grew up as a coach stop on the road north, then around the Royal Hunting Lodge which became the site of magnificent Blenheim Palace – the home of the dukes of Marlborough since the early 1700s.

At the centre of Woodstock the superb town hall stands proud at the apex of a triangle formed with High Street on one side, Market Street on the other and Oxford Street at the base. The ancient town is a popular antiques and artworks centre attracting many visitors. There are some 20 pubs, inns and hotels. If you stroll to Park Lane you can see Thomas Chaucer's Cottage. Thomas was the son of poet Geoffrey Chaucer (1345–1400), author of *The Canterbury Tales*, and like his father he sat in Parliament, becoming the Speaker in the House of Commons.

The Black Prince

The Black Prince is a truly unique pub offering an excellent choice of real ales and an exciting French-inspired menu. It is a delight to sit out in the award-winning riverside garden looking down on the River Glyme, which flows into Blenheim Park to form Queen Lake, and across to the Water Meadows Nature Reserve opposite. Well known in the area, the Black Prince has regularly featured in the *Good Pub Guide*. Walkers are made very welcome. There is a varied menu which includes Mexican dishes and pizzas. To enjoy a pizza in the riverside garden, with a glass of Thatcher's cider in hand is my version of Utopia. Telephone: 01993 811530.

THE WALK

Leave the **Hensington Road** car park at the rear and head right along the backs of houses to a road junction. Turn right along a metalled lane heading north past **Woodstock cemetery**. The lane soon becomes a hedged path. After walking the path for about 1 mile, go through a gate onto the B4027 road. Turn left along the grass verge of this quiet lane until you reach the crossroads by **Sansoms Cottages**.

Turn left through the kissing-gate on the corner and walk the clear path over cultivated land. Go through the hand-gate and bear right to a further gate. Now go left, crossing a footbridge, to reach another gate and open land. There is a pleasant valley view to the right with a pond and the **River Dorn** below – the village of **Wootton** can be seen on the hill opposite. Bear left through a garden to reach a wide track at a junction of paths. Cross over the track and proceed south on a footpath to the right of the field hedge. Maintain your direction over three fields where you will see wild poppies flowering in the summer months. After crossing a couple of stiles you reach **Stratford Lane**.

Drive and Stroll

Strolling up to the Grand Bridge in

 3

Turn right along the lane to reach a junction of roads, where you bear left to the A44. Cross over the busy road with care and go through the gate opposite, walking the **Oxfordshire Way** to a second gate and onto a farm track. Turn right, then go left over a stile onto a clear path, aiming for a stile set to the right of **Furze Platt**. Continue over a further stile and go through the farm gate.

 4

Some 230 yards beyond the farm gate, turn left and walk along the straight tarmac drive (now going south-east) through **Blenheim Park** – the **Column of Victory** will be ahead. After ½ mile of easy walking, the drive arcs left and leads down to the edge of **Queen Pool**, but you continue ahead up a sheep track to visit the huge column and then descend to the superb **Grand Bridge** to enjoy a fine view of the impressive north frontage of **Blenheim Palace**.

The name of the palace derives from a famous battle that took place on 13 August 1704 on the north bank of the River Danube, where John Churchill, the first Duke of Marlborough, won a great victory over the forces of the French king, Louis XIV, during the War of the Spanish Succession. The Column of Victory was erected to commemorate the event. Queen Anne rewarded Marlborough with the Royal manor of Woodstock and built him this fine house. It has been the home of the Churchill family ever since, and Sir Winston Churchill, our wartime leader, was born here in 1874. The park was designed by Capability Brown in the 1760s.

 (5)

Turn left along the tarmac park road, passing to the left of **Queen Pool**. At the end of the pool turn right, going over a small bridge, then bear left to leave the tarmac drive, walking along a footpath up to a gate set to the left of a cottage, with a conservatory. Proceed through the gate, passing between houses to reach the A44 in **Woodstock**. Cross over the A44 with care, pass through the kissing gate and bear right over the footbridge along a clear signed footpath to the right of the **River Glyme** – the **Black Prince** is on the far bank of the river. This footpath will lead you back to the car park.

PLACES OF INTEREST NEARBY

While you are here, it would be a pity not to visit **Blenheim Palace** itself, today the home of the 11th Duke of Marlborough. It is a World Heritage Site and a masterpiece of architecture by Vanbrugh. Telephone: 01993 811091. Website: www.blenheimpalace.com.

 Bladon, 3 miles south, is an historic village whose church is the final resting place of Sir Winston Churchill, who was buried there in a family grave in 1965.

8 Begbroke and Bladon

The entrance to the woods on

The Walk 5¼ miles
Terrain An easy walk on good footpaths and farm tracks
Map OS Explorer 180 Oxford (GR 468129)

How to get there

Begbroke is on the A44, 5½ miles north-west of Oxford. Turn left off the main road up Spring Hill Road, then right into St Michael's Lane. **Parking:** In St Michael's Lane in Begbroke.

Introduction

From the pretty village of Begbroke, this interesting walk takes you through some lovely countryside to Bladon, where our great wartime Prime Minister, Winston Churchill, is buried. Begbroke had just nine tenants at the time of the Domesday Book in 1086, and this number had increased only to 13 by 1279, but archaeological evidence shows that people had lived in this area for centuries before that. You pass Round Castle, a plateau hill fort, and the stroll continues into the woodland on Bladon Heath, where you can enjoy the

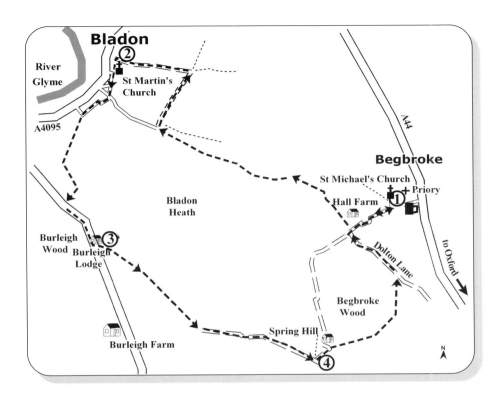

butterflies and flowers and hear woodland birds (in spring there is a spectacular show of bluebells). At Bladon the route goes past the churchyard and the great man's gravestone, and you return down the ancient Dolton Lane.

The Royal Sun

The Royal Sun has been a hostelry for over 300 years. It was originally called the Rising Sun and then, following a royal visit in the days of Charles II, it was renamed the Royal Sun. This was probably the 'disorderly house' being reported to the magistrates in 1711 and 1745; there were also problems in 1723 because Hannah Graves, the wife of the landlord John, was placed in the stocks for causing a disturbance in the village – John himself was fined £40 for being disorderly! Today, this historic pub is a peaceful place offering generous portions of popular dishes, including hand-carved gammon ham, eggs and chips, sandwiches, baguettes, wraps and jacket potatoes all at reasonable prices. Telephone: 01865 372231.

Drive and Stroll

THE WALK

(1)

Leave **St Michael's Lane**, turn right past the old school building and proceed up **Spring Hill Road**, passing through the old part of **Begbroke village**. Just past the **Hall Farm complex** you arrive at the entrance to a house called **Village End**. Turn right along the clearly signed bridlepath to **Bladon**. Initially this is a somewhat narrow path by the side of the driveway to the house, then a bridlegate takes you onto a wide grass farm track by a field hedge. Walk along the edge of this field and then enter the superb woodland of **Bladon Heath** via another bridlegate.

Round Castle, on Bladon Heath, may be an Iron Age fortification, though finds such as flints, scrapers, arrowheads, a polished axe-head and a piece of 2nd-century pottery indicate an even earlier settlement.

Stroll along the good clear track through the mainly deciduous woodland. As you approach the end of the wood there are some conifer trees and then a final bridlegate leads up onto a grass area. Follow the clear footpath to the edge of **Bladon village** where you will emerge by a row of lock-up garages. Then turn right down a grass track set to the left of a field hedge, passing more woodland. At the bottom of the field turn left along the grass track to the right of the field hedge to arrive in the village. The track becomes a tarmac lane and you pass by some attractive large houses.

  (2)

Turn left into the churchyard of **St Martin's church** in **Bladon**, passing the Churchill family graves. Leave the churchyard via the lychgate and stroll along **Church Street** to the lovely village green. Continue ahead along Church Street and at the road junction continue into **Manor Road**. This road bends sharp right past attractive new cottages and then bends left to a stile and open countryside. Initially there will be a hedge to your right and you descend gently by this. Near the end of this hedgerow there is another hedge coming in from the left and then the footpath arcs left along the side of a ditch. In about 200 yards turn right over a narrow footbridge and ascend by the side of a field hedge to reach a road. Turn left along the road for another 200 yards.

  (3)

Immediately after passing **Burleigh Lodge**, turn left over a stile onto a clear footpath signed 'Yarnton', noting the millennium stone. Initially you walk by trees and then cross a cultivated field to continue to the left of the next field hedge. Continue along the good path over several fields, passing a lovely old oak tree where you bear left onto a grass track set to the right of the field hedge.

The historic Royal Sun in Begbroke

After passing through another gap, the track begins to gently ascend and as you near the top there is a gap in the hedge.

  (4)

Turn left towards the building on **Spring Hill**. Just before you reach the house, turn right through a farm gateway and descend the farm track (a public footpath) past **Begbroke Wood**. The track arcs left through a hedge gap into pastureland. Cross the pasture, aiming for another hedge gap in the far corner. Turn left along the hedged grass track of **Dolton Lane**.

Dolton Lane is believed to have been part of an ancient route – it was called Green Lane in 1844.

Ignore the footpath going off to the right and walk **Dolton Lane** to its end (about ¼ mile). Just after passing a partly-timbered cottage, bear right into **Spring Hill Road** and descend into **Begbroke**. Stroll past **Hall Farm** and retrace your steps back to **St Michael's Lane**. The **Royal Sun** is at the bottom of the hedged road.

PLACES OF INTEREST NEARBY

Oxford, the 'city of dreaming spires', is just 5 miles away to the south-east. Stroll the ancient city streets and enjoy seeing some of the most beautiful college buildings in the world. Contact the Tourist Information Office for further information on 01865 726871; or visit www.oxford.gov.uk/tourism

9 Minster Lovell and the River Windrush

The romantic ruins of Minster Lovell Hall

The Walk 3¼ miles
Terrain Good footpaths and tracks
Map OS Explorer 180 Oxford (GR 318111)

How to get there

Minster Lovell is situated about 15 miles west of Oxford. From the A40 turn right at Bushey Ground, following the signs into the village. **Parking:** Wash Meadow car park is just over the bridge as you enter the village.

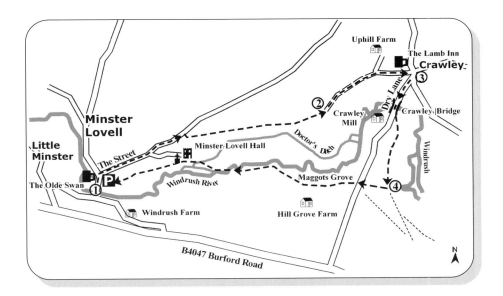

Introduction

A row of beautiful thatched cottages lines the main street of ancient Minster Lovell and there are fine views to enjoy as you stroll above the Windrush river into the nearby village of Crawley. The return route is along the river bank and you will pass by the superb ruins of Minster Lovell Hall, and the 15th-century church. At the time of the Domesday Book, in 1086, there were two manors at Minstre and Parva Minstre (Little Minster) and these were separated by the river, with a toll bridge between. The river provided fish for food, marshland for gamefowl and reeds for thatching. In the 20th century the village was well known for its good quality rushes, which were used for caulking barrels and for roofing.

The Olde Swan Inn

This attractive hotel offers a satisfying blend of Cotswold half-timbering and slate. It is very popular with Oxford students, who celebrate here on completion of their exams. Sir Winston Churchill was a regular visitor and another prime minister, Harold Wilson and his wife Mary spent their honeymoon here. The notorious highwaymen Tom, Dick and Harry also stopped here! Walkers are assured of a warm welcome and the inn is open from 11 am to 11 pm each day. Food is available at lunchtime throughout the week between 12 noon and 2.30 pm and in the evenings between 7 pm and 9 pm (9.30 pm on Friday and

Drive and Stroll

Saturday). A full bar menu is offered, with tasty items from the restaurant menu. There is an attractive garden. Telephone: 01993 774441.

THE WALK

(1)

Leave **Wash Meadow** car park via the field gate entrance and go right past the **Olde Swan Inn**. Then turn right again to stroll up the main street (known as **The Street**) of **Old Minster**, taking time to enjoy the picture postcard scene of 16th- and 17th-century thatched Cotswold stone cottages – a number with house names that reveal their historic uses. Continue past the signed turn-off to **Minster Lovell Hall** – you will visit this on the return journey – and in about 120 yards turn right over a stile onto a signed footpath towards **Crawley**, walking across pastureland. To the right there is a good view of the ruins of **Minster Lovell Hall** and a particularly fine dovecote. Initially aim for a second stile in the hedge ahead and then progress by the side of the hedge/fence, walking over several fields and going over a series of stiles. After about ½ mile of pleasant walking, go over a stile into a narrow cattle enclosure and leave this via a gate to ascend a hedged track – there are pleasing views to the right, the **Windrush valley** with **Crawley village** and its mill standing out.

 (2)

A second gate takes you onto a lane, which leads up to a T-junction of lanes. Go right – this is **Farm Lane** and you pass in front of **Rose Cottage** before descending into the pretty village of **Crawley**. The **Lamb Inn** is to the left as you reach the road junction.

 (3)

Turn right along the pavement of **Dry Lane**, enjoying the many tiny bridges that allow access to cottages on the banks of the village stream. Continue down **Dry Lane** and cross over the **Windrush** river bridge, but take care as it is very narrow. Some 12 yards beyond the bridge turn left through a gate and now walk a hedged footpath (signed '**Circular Walk Bridlepath – Witney**'), passing through pleasant pastureland.

 (4)

In about 550 yards proceed through two gates and go right to ascend the path to another gate to arrive back on **Dry Lane**. Cross the lane and go through the metal kissing-gate opposite, then continue on the path (now signed '**Circular Walk Foopath – Minster Lovell**') to reach a further stile into trees. Descend the path through the trees to another stile at its end and then walk by the side of the **River Windrush**, going over a series of fields and stiles. Yet another stile leads into an area of trees and the path meanders through these to arrive at a footbridge/stile over the river. From here there is a fine view of the ruins of **Minster Lovell Hall**,

The Olde Swan in Minster Lovell

the dovecote and **St Kenelm's church**.

The old hall is an English Heritage site and you can take this opportunity to explore the various buildings (entrance is free and the buildings are open at all reasonable times). William Lovell built the manor house and the church in 1431. He died in 1455 and is commemorated in *St Kenelm's. The hall passed to his son and later was inherited by Francis, Lord Lovell, but changed ownership many times after that.*

Enter the churchyard and depart via the stile in the west wall to walk the path through the fields at the back of the cottages in **The Street**. You will soon reach the recreation area and the car park in **Wash Meadow**.

PLACES OF INTEREST NEARBY

The **Cotswold Wildlife Park and Gardens**, 6 miles to the west, offers a super day out for the family. As well as lions, leopards, rhinos and other animals from around the world, the park has 160 acres of parkland and gardens to explore. Telephone: 01993 823006.

10 | Horspath and Shotover Country Park

St Giles' church in Horspath

The Walk 3 miles
Terrain Good footpaths, country lanes and farm tracks.
Map OS Explorer 180 Oxford (GR 571048)

How to get there

Horspath is about 3 miles south-east of Oxford. Leave Oxford on the A420 London road. Turn right onto the Eastern Bypass road (the A4142). Then turn left along Horspath Road and finally bear left into Horspath village. **Parking:** With consideration by the roadside near to St Giles' church in Horspath.

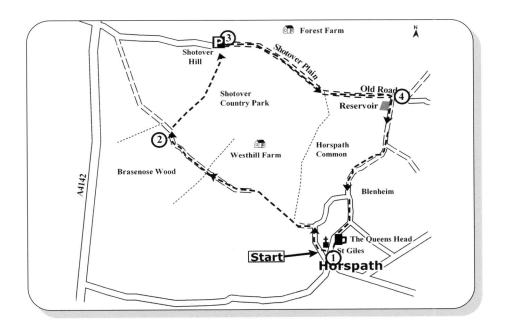

Introduction

Country tracks take you from the village of Horspath, which nestles on the slopes of Shotover Hill, up into the woodland of Shotover Country Park and along the Shotover Plain before you descend on a peaceful path back into Horspath. It was the old bridlepath joining the London Road through Wheatley that gave the village its Anglo-Saxon name of Horsepadan, which became Horsepath, but in 1912 the parish council reverted to the unique form, Horspath. In days gone by much of the surrounding land was owned by the influential Oxford colleges of Corpus Christi, Magdalen and Brasenose, evidence of which remains in the name of Brasenose Wood.

The Queen's Head

The Queen's Head in Church Street is a typical English pub. In 1936 it caught fire and sparks from its then thatched roof destroyed two cottages opposite – it was restored with a tiled roof. Today the pub offers a good range of reasonably priced bar meals, including sandwiches, baguettes and jacket potatoes, which can be enjoyed in its large garden. During the week it is open from 12 noon to 3 pm and from 5 pm to 11 pm, and then on Friday and at weekends it is open

Drive and Stroll

all day from 12 noon to 11 pm (10.30 pm on Sunday). Snacks are served during the week between 12 noon and 2 pm (3 pm on Saturday) and between 5 pm and 8 pm in the evenings. The Sunday roast is rather special and is served between 1 pm and 3 pm. Telephone: 01865 875567.

THE WALK

From **St Giles' church** stroll into **Manor Farm Road** and turn right. Just before the entrance to the farm itself, turn left along the signed footpath. As this path arcs left, continue ahead and go through the kissing-gate into farmland. Proceed across the field with the trees of **Shotover Country Park** up to your right. Continue through another kissing-gate into the next field and now stroll ahead along a wide grass verge. The next two fields are used as 'set aside' land and you can enjoy a superb display of wildflowers, with the buildings of **Westhill Farm** visible below the trees. The path becomes a clear track as you enter the edge of **Brasenose Wood**, and you may be lucky enough to see a fox.

After walking this track through the trees for about 450 yards, bear right. Go under a metal barrier and stroll up a hedged footpath towards **Shotover Country Park**.

Shotover was a Royal Forest from the time of the Domesday Book until 1660, when it was in such poor condition that it was removed from

the jurisdiction of the Forest Laws. A connection with Queen's College comes from the 1400s, when a student named John Copcot was walking in the forest. He was attacked by a wild boar, but managed to thrust the copy of Aristotle that he had been reading down the boar's throat, with the result that 'the boar expired'. The event is commemorated at the College by the ceremony of 'carrying in the boar's head' at Christmas, and by a window in St Giles' church in Horspath.

Soon you will be walking up a clear track through the lovely woodland. Follow the main track up through the superb oak and other deciduous trees. After a general ascent of about 200 yards you bear left to arrive on **Shotover Hill**, at the car park.

Turn right and stroll along the wide sandy track called **Shotover Plain**. This is easy walking in generally open surroundings and will enable you to recover your breath after the ascent. If you wish to move off the sandy track you can do so, keeping in the same direction.

This wide sandy track became a turnpike under the Stokenchurch Turnpike Act of 1719, the

Interesting tree shapes in Shotover Park

introduction to the act stating that it had 'become so Ruinous and Bad, that in the winter season the said Road is Dangerous to Travellers.'

After about ½ mile of level walking, you will pass a footpath coming up from the right through the trees and can soon go through a hedge gap to walk over a set-aside field on the other side of the hedge. In about 300 yards as you approach the mound of a reservoir, leave the field via another gap and continue along the sandy track of **Shotover Plain**. In a few yards you will see the reservoir.

 ④

Immediately after passing the reservoir, turn right down **Blenheim Road** – another sandy track. It descends to reach the end of woodland on **Horspath Common** where you can remain on the 'road' or enter the trees at the proper gap and walk the footpath that runs parallel with it. Continue into the village of **Horspath**, bearing left to descend into **Church Road**. As you progress you walk past **the Queen's Head pub** and then arrive back at **St Giles' church**.

PLACES OF INTEREST NEARBY

Waterperry Gardens, near Wheatley, just to the east of Horspath, are well worth a visit. This 8-acre garden, open all year round, is famed for its herbaceous borders. There is also a museum, garden shop and tearoom. Telephone: 01844 339254.

11 | Wootton and Boars Hill

Jarn Mound commemorates the work of Matthew Arnold

The Walk 3½ miles
Terrain An easy walk on good footpaths and bridleways
Map OS Explorer 180 Oxford (GR 486022)

How to get there

Boars Hill is about 3 miles south-west of Oxford. Leaving Oxford on the A420, turn left onto the A34 Southern Bypass and at the A423 junction take the second exit into Hinksey Hill. Turn right into Foxcombe Road and right again into Berkeley Road then left into Jarn Way. **Parking:** In the small parking area near to Jarn Mound, in Jarn Way.

Drive and Stroll

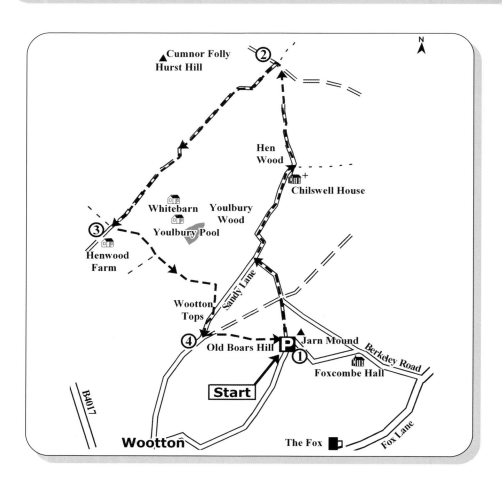

Introduction

This is a delightful historic walk through the Oxfordshire countryside, offering views over the city of Oxford. The walk starts from the Jarn Mound (administered by the Oxford Preservation Trust), which is surrounded by a Wild Garden created by Sir Arthur Evans. The route continues into Youlbury Woods, passing the International Scout Camp and Chilswell House, where Robert Bridges (1844-1930) lived and died. He was the Poet Laureate from 1913 to 1930 and his former home is now a retreat run by a community of Carmelite friars. On into lovely countryside and you will soon be walking along a peaceful farm lane to return to Boars Hill.

The Fox Inn

Situated near the edge of the rural village of Boars Hill, this traditional inn has wooden beams and open fires, and its welcoming ambiance and good food make for a very happy visit. Outside, attractive floral displays greet customers during the summer and there is a beer garden. There is a reasonably priced menu of sandwiches, light meals, hot crusty baguettes and jacket potatoes to appeal to the traveller in a hurry. The Fox is open during the day from Monday to Saturday 11 am to 2.30 pm and on Sunday from 12 noon to 2.30 pm, and in the evenings from 6 pm to 11 pm. Food is available every day of the week between 12 noon and 2.30 pm and from 6.30 pm to 9 pm in the evenings. Telephone: 01865 735131.

THE WALK

From the parking area, spare time before you start the walk to go up the steps to **Jarn Mound**.

Jarn Mound is an artificial mound built in the 1930s at the personal expense of Sir Arthur John Evans (1851–1941) to commemorate the work of the poet Matthew Arnold (1822–1888) and to provide a viewpoint over Oxford. To prevent encroachment by development, it was surrounded by a Wild Garden. Evans had a house on Boars Hill called 'Youlbury', now demolished.

In about 300 yards you reach a junction of lanes. Continue ahead over the junction and in a further 300 yards arrive at **Sandy Lane**. Here bear right along the quiet and pleasant lane towards **Chilswell House** and the **International Scout Camp**. Do not go up the private driveway to the house but bear left and then right, still aiming towards the **Scout Camp Reception**. You will pass to the left of the house and enjoy a pleasing view of the building through the trees to the right. After you pass the Reception area the lane becomes a sandy track and descends though delightful woodland – a carpet of bluebells in spring – until you reach the edge of **Hen Wood**. A hand-gate leads into the open and a clear pathway takes you to another hand-gate onto a good track. Turn left along the track for about 50 yards to a junction of paths.

Turn left and stroll along the clear farm track with **Hurst Hill** up to your right. Walk along this track for about 1 mile.

About 450 yards after passing by a small copse on the left, turn left and go over a stile into pastureland. This

Drive and Stroll

The Fox at Boars Hill

signed footpath soon hugs the right-hand edge of the field, with the houses of the hamlet of **Whitebarn** up to your left. Go over the stiles and footbridge at the field end and continue along the signed path by the hedge to a further pair of stiles and a footbridge. Go over these and continue ahead towards a stile in the trees. Enter the woodland, ascending the lovely footpath through a carpet of bluebells in spring, or foxgloves in summer. After about 300 yards, cross the driveway to a large house and

then turn right to walk along a hedged path, passing houses, to reach **Sandy Lane**. Turn right and descend the quiet lane for 175 yards to a junction with the road.

  (4)

Turn sharp left, proceed up the track and in a few yards you will reach a bridlegate. Go through this and stroll down over the commonland, going through a second bridlegate. The path arcs right around the edge of a fenced area and then you ascend, over the pastureland of **Matthew Arnold's Field**, to reach a kissing-gate.

The Oxford Preservation Trust administers two sites on Old Boars Hill – Jarn Mound and Matthew Arnold's Field. Arnold, one of our greatest poets, was professor of Poetry at Oxford from 1857 to 1867.

Go through the kissing-gate and bear left along a driveway to stroll back to the parking area.

PLACES OF INTEREST NEARBY

Oxford Castle is well worth a visit. Learn the history of its turbulent past and climb St George's Tower for a 360° panoramic view of the city. It is open every day of the year except Christmas Day. Telephone: 01865 260666; www.oxfordcastleunlocked.co.uk

Drive and Stroll

12 | The Ridgeway near Watlington

The view down Shirburn Hill

The Walk 4 miles
Terrain Well walked footpaths, including part of the Ridgeway
Map OS Explorer 171 Chiltern Hills West (GR 725955)

How to get there

From Junction 5 on the M40, follow the A40 north towards Oxford for 1 mile. Turn off left at the television mast, following the sign to the Sculpture Trail. Continue for 2 miles, over the motorway, and find Cowleaze Wood on the left. **Parking:** Cowleaze Wood car park.

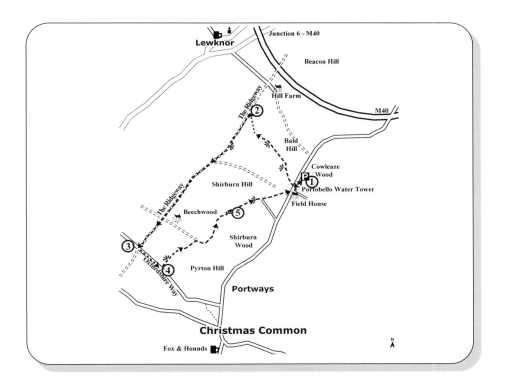

Introduction

There are many fine views to enjoy on this lovely stroll. You will pass through attractive coniferous woodland near to Bald Hill and walk a beautiful stretch of the famous Ridgeway. A quiet country lane takes you over the Access Land of Shirburn Hill on the return to Cowleaze Wood, where you are likely to see the magnificent red kites which were reintroduced to the Chilterns area in the 1990s. Christmas Common, where the Fox and Hounds pub is situated, got its name from an incident during the Civil War when Royalists and Parliamentarians squared up to each other at Christmas 1643 – but even Cromwell wanted a rest on Christmas Day and a truce was quickly called.

The Fox and Hounds

This old pub dates back to the 16th century but it was not until 1896 that Brakspear's acquired the property. The Fox and Hounds is a friendly pub where the very best food is offered. From Monday to Friday it is open between 12 noon

Drive and Stroll

and 3.30 pm and in the evenings between 5.30 pm and 11 pm; all day at weekends from 11 am to 10.30 pm. From 12 noon to 2.30 pm a bar menu is offered including sandwiches. In the evenings between 7 pm and 9.30 pm an 'à la carte' menu offers outstanding food which is generally modern British organic and local fare – it has been known to attract a national celebrity or two. There is a pleasant garden area where children are allowed. Dogs on leads and under strict control are allowed in the bar and the garden. Walkers who are customers may use the car park. Telephone: 01491 612599.

THE WALK

From **Cowleaze Wood** car park, head southwards through the trees towards the **Portobello Water Tower**. Leave the woodland here, cross over the road and then pass through the bridlegate opposite into **Aston Rowant Nature Reserve**. Soon you will pass through another gateway and then descend more steeply through a narrow strip of trees. In about 150 yards the pathway bends right and then left to continue along a good footpath into an open area with pleasing views down the valley and towards **Bald Hill**. Follow the clear white-painted path signs, passing through a couple of further bridlegates, then walk to the left of **Old Cricketground Plantation**. About halfway down the side, turn right through a hand-gate into the plantation and follow the footpath through the attractive trees. Soon you will emerge from the other end of the plantation and cross a field to arrive on the **Ridgeway**.

This famous long-distance footpath stretches some 87 miles through the North Wessex Downs and the Chilterns, both Areas of Outstanding Natural Beauty.

Turn left along the very wide hedged track – up to your left is the lovely **Bald Hill**. As you continue along the track you pass through the bottom end of some coniferous trees and will soon see the farm complex of **Beechwood** to your left, set amid beech trees. Continue along the hedge-lined track for about 1 mile until you reach a quiet country lane with a 'Way' sign at a meeting of the **Ridgeway** and the **Oxfordshire Way**.

Turn left along the **Oxfordshire Way** and stroll up the lane for about ¼ mile.

The Oxfordshire Way is a 65-mile walking route between Bourton-on-the-Water and Henley-on-Thames.

About 50 yards after passing some white fencing, turn left up a signed footpath into an area of bushes.

Ridgeway track below Shirburn Hill

Follow the nicely grassed track (the footpath does bend away from this) and in about 400 yards you will reach a junction of footpaths and waymarks. Bear right up the footpath by the side of the field edge. To your left are some of the buildings at **Beechwood** and, as you continue along the field edge for the next ½ mile, you can enjoy pleasing views to the left over the undulating countryside. Eventually a public footpath sign veers you right and you arrive at a kissing-gate below the access land of **Shirburn Hill**.

 (5)

Go through the kissing-gate and follow the very clear footpath route (over some mole hills). Soon you will be ascending rather steeply, to emerge in the trees. Continue to the very top of the hill and bear left over a field corner stile (there are some railway sleeper steps). Follow the waymarker direction and diagonally cross the pastureland to reach a stile onto the road opposite **Field House**. Bear left and then cross the road to re-enter **Cowleaze Wood** and retrace your steps back to the car park.

PLACES OF INTEREST NEARBY

Wallingford, 6 miles to the south-west, is a beautiful old historic town that was granted its charter in 1155. Walk through the castle gardens where you can still make out some of the ancient fortifications and walk down to the river to view the medieval bridge that spans the Thames. Telephone: 01491 835373; www.wallingfordtown.co.uk

13 Buscot and Kelmscott

Narrow boats on the River Thames near Kelmscott

The Walk 5 miles
Terrain Good footpaths and tracks
Map OS Explorer 170 Abingdon, Wantage and Vale of the White Horse (GR 232976)

How to get there

Buscot is 4 miles north-west of Faringdon along the A417 Lechlade road. Turn off the A417 into the village. **Parking:** Buscot Weir car park.

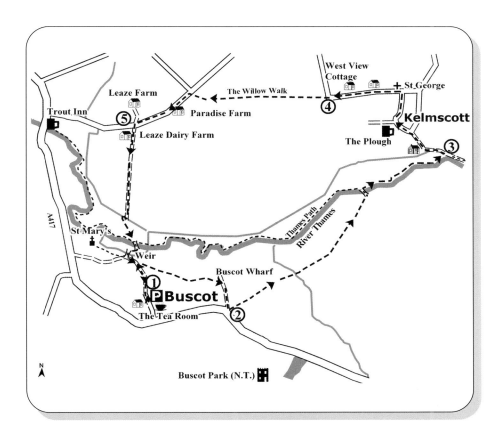

Introduction

The walk starts in the delightful village of Buscot. You will stroll across lovely Oxfordshire countryside and along part of the Thames Path, then through the superb village of Kelmscott made famous by its associations with William Morris (1834–1896), the poet and craftsman whose influence on design and textiles is still felt today. Further field walking brings you back towards Buscot where you cross over Buscot Weir and have the opportunity of visiting St Mary's church before returning to your car. Buscot is a National Trust village which originally developed around the church but, following the 14th-century Black Death and the enclosure of land for sheep, moved away from St Mary's and then expanded in the mid 19th century to accommodate a growing estate workforce. You will pass the oldest buildings at the entrance to the village and a little further along the A417 road is the 17th-century manor, set apart from the main settlement.

Drive and Stroll

The Plough Inn

In Kelmscott you will be assured of a warm welcome at the Plough Inn, which was built in 1631 near to Kelmscott Manor. Several real ales are on tap and a wide choice of wines is available by the bottle or the glass. Food is available throughout the week and dishes may include homemade steak and kidney pudding, lasagne, local game pie, Kelmscott ham, egg and chips and fish platter. In the evening a full à la carte menu is offered. Serving times are 12 noon to 2.30 pm and 7 pm to 9 pm (9.30 pm at weekends). This is a popular pub and booking is essential for Sunday lunch. There is a pleasant garden area and dogs are allowed in the garden and in the bar if under strict control. Telephone: 01367 253543; email plough@kelmscottg17.fsnet.co.uk

THE WALK

(1)

Turn right out of the car park to walk the lane towards **Buscot Weir**. Just before you reach the weir, turn right again and go over a stile onto a clear footpath, walking to the left of the field hedge with the **River Thames** to the far left. At the end of the field the path veers right, through to the other side of the hedge, and you continue past a cottage to reach a farm track. Here, turn right and stroll up the track to reach the A417 road.

 (2)

Do not go onto the road but turn sharp left through a metal gate and walk the clear, well-used footpath across a cultivated field. Continue ahead, walking the length of the long field and you will soon reach a small footbridge over a stream. Go over this and turn right, then go left up a farm track set to the right of the next field hedge. The track ascends and then descends into the next field. Continue to the left along the field and within a few yards you will reach a junction of footpaths. Turn left and follow the clear footpath over a long, cultivated field until you arrive at a farm track. Turn left and stroll down to **Old Hart's Weir**. Proceed past the former keeper's cottage and go over the footbridge. Now turn right and join the **Thames Path** footpath, following this into the village of **Kelmscott**. This is lovely walking on a fine day. You pass a Second World War bunker. Proceed over the footbridge onto the track on the edge of **Kelmscott**.

 (3)

Turn left to stroll up into this attractive village. Within a few yards you will pass **Kelmscott Manor**.

Kelmscott Manor was the home for 25 years of the designer William Morris and the village has many reminders of his influence locally and nationally.

Buscot Weir

Bear left at a road junction, past a fascinating house where a sculpted picture of William Morris on the wall will catch the eye. Soon you pass the **Plough Inn**, as you walk along the quiet village street up to a road junction. Turn left past the delightful church of **St George**, where you can find the grave of William Morris in the churchyard. Continue along the road, passing attractive houses and cottages. Shortly after passing **West View Cottage**, you will reach a bend in the road.

  (4)

Here you leave the road and continue ahead on a clear, well-used footpath across a cultivated field. Go over a small footbridge and soon you are walking a wide track set to the left of the field hedge (the **Willow Walk**). Go over the stile at the field end and continue ahead to a final stile onto the road, set to the right of **Paradise Farm**. Turn left and stroll along the generally quiet road for about 550 yards. You pass **Paradise Farm** and then the entrance driveway to **Leaze Farm** (on the right).

Drive and Stroll

5

Just after passing this turn, go left up the public footpath towards **Leaze Dairy Farm**. It becomes a fenced farm track and you will enjoy the open views along this good wide track towards a row of tall trees. The footpath turns sharp right just before the trees and then left over a couple of small footbridges. As you emerge from the trees, bear left towards **Buscot Lock** on the **River Thames**. Cross over the lock gates and bear right to go over a further footbridge, past the keeper's cottage and to reach the entrance drive. Walk back along this good track, which becomes a tarmac road as you arrive back in **Buscot** village.

PLACES OF INTEREST NEARBY

Buscot Park (National Trust) is the 17th-century home of the Faringdon family, with a walled garden and lovely grounds. Website: www.nationaltrust.org.uk

Kelmscott Manor, a Grade I listed Tudor farmhouse, adjacent to the River Thames, is now owned and managed by the Society of Antiquaries and is open on some days in summer. Telephone: 01367 252486.

14 | Badbury Hill and the Great Barn

The Great Barn at Great Coxwell

The Walk 5½ miles
Terrain An easy walk along good footpaths and farm tracks
Map OS Explorer 170 Abingdon, Wantage and Vale of the White Horse (GR 262945)

How to get there

Badbury Hill is about 3 miles west of Faringdon on the B4019. Parking: In the free National Trust car park at Badbury Hill on the B4019, just past the Holloway Road turning into Great Coxwell.

Drive and Stroll

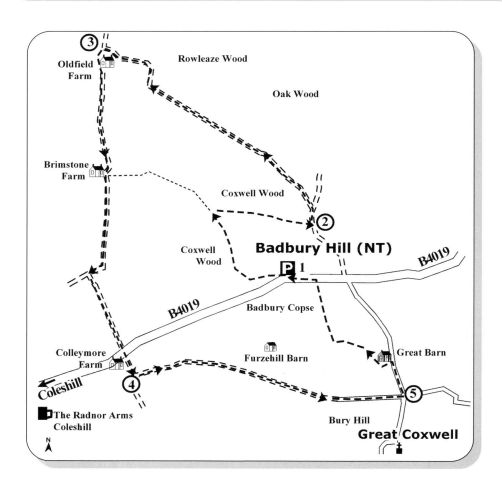

Introduction

A delightful walk from the National Trust's Badbury Hill, which today is an attractive area of mainly beech trees. Some 2,500 years ago it was the site of an Iron Age settlement, though the exposed sandy outcrop has been eroded over time. It was largely levelled early in the 19th century, but the circular earthen rampart and ditch are still visible. Can you imagine the enclosed round huts, storage pits for grain and pens for livestock? The route takes you over attractive countryside to the historic village of Great Coxwell, where you can visit St Giles' church, before passing through the grounds of the National Trust's impressive Great Barn on its way back to Badbury Hill.

The Radnor Arms

The Radnor Arms was originally the village smithy at Coleshill (2 miles west on the B4109), but was changed by local workers to a village pub in 1949 – it still retains a good display of farming and blacksmith's tools in the 'Smithy' bar. The pub is owned by the National Trust and is built on a split level. It has become a popular 'local' serving beers from casks behind the bar – normally the ales on tap are from local breweries within a 25 mile range of the pub. The Radnor Arms is open every lunch time between 11 am (noon on Sunday) and 3 pm and in the evenings from 6 pm to 11 pm (10.30 pm on Sunday). Food is available between noon and 2 pm each day, when you can enjoy your meal in the pleasing gardens, and in the evenings between 7 pm and 9 pm – no food is served on Monday or on Sunday evening. Telephone: 01793 861575.

THE WALK

From the car park proceed over the stile into the main area of woodland and stroll along the clear wide footpath into the trees. After about ½ mile you reach a junction of footpaths. Here, turn right and leave the **Badbury Hill** area via a further stile. Continue through the undergrowth and in about 150 yards bear right onto a footpath coming in from the left. This footpath hugs the edge of the woodland with a view of the trees on **Badbury Hill** to your right. After re-entering the trees you reach a lane.

Head left along the lane to a farm gate. Go over the stile to the left of the gate and bear left along a pleasant green track set to the right of the woodland. Follow the waymark signs as the track arcs right and then left to become hedged. At the end of the trees bear left over a stile and aim towards **Oldfield Farm**. At the farm gate, go through the kissing-gate and walk the bridlepath past a row of terraced farm cottages to join a path that arcs left to reach the main farm complex. Continue along the track to the right of the farm buildings.

Bear left and walk along the concrete driveway up to **Brimstone Farm**. Bear left onto the access road and proceed along this road for almost a mile until you arrive at the main road near to **Colleymore Farm**. Cross over and continue ahead along the lane/bridleway signed to **Great Coxwell**. In about 200 yards you reach a track junction.

Bear left onto a broad track over open pastureland. This soon becomes a hedged track. Then, as you begin to approach **Great Coxwell**, it becomes a lane (**Puddleduck**

Drive and Stroll

Lane) which leads to the main road in the village.

 ⑤

Turn left through the village – the **church of St Giles** is to the right if you wish to look round. Stroll through the village until you reach the **Great Barn**, set back to the left.

The massive Great Barn was built in Cotswold stone in the 13th century – it is 152 ft long and 44 ft wide, and 48 ft up to the ridge. There was a cell here of the Cistercian abbey at Beaulieu and, after the dissolution of the monasteries in the 16th century, it passed to the Mores family, eventually becoming part of the Coleshill estate owned by the Pleydell-Bouverie family (the Radnor Earls). In 1956 it was bequeathed to the National Trust by Mr E. E. Cook, who had purchased it in 1945 and it is free to enter.

Leave the **Great Barn** via the gateway at the rear. Bear right along

St Giles' church in Great Coxwell

the field edge and enter woodland over a stile. When a final stile takes you out of the woodland, bear right until you reach the B4019. At the road, turn left to return to **Badbury Hill** car park.

PLACES OF INTEREST NEARBY

Coleshill, 2 miles away to the west, contains many fine Cotswold stone houses looking down over the River Cole and the Wiltshire border. Sadly, the 17th-century Coleshill House, home of the Pleydell-Bouverie family, burned down in 1952, but substantial buildings remain in this beautiful village and there is an old mill on the banks of the Cole that is administered by the National Trust. Telephone (NT estate office): 01793 762209. Website: www.nationaltrust.org.uk/buscotandcoleshill

15 | Little Wittenham and The Clumps

The River Thames at Little Wittenham

The Walk 6 miles
Terrain An easy walk on good paths
Map OS Explorer 170 Abingdon, Wantage and Vale of the White Horse
(GR 567923)

How to get there

Little Wittenham is near the small town of Dorchester. From the A415 Abingdon road at Clifton Hampden, turn south following the signs for Long Wittenham but before you get into the village turn left for Little Wittenham. Turn right in the village and follow the country lane past Hill Farm. **Parking:** In the free parking area about 500 yards past Hill Farm.

Drive and Stroll

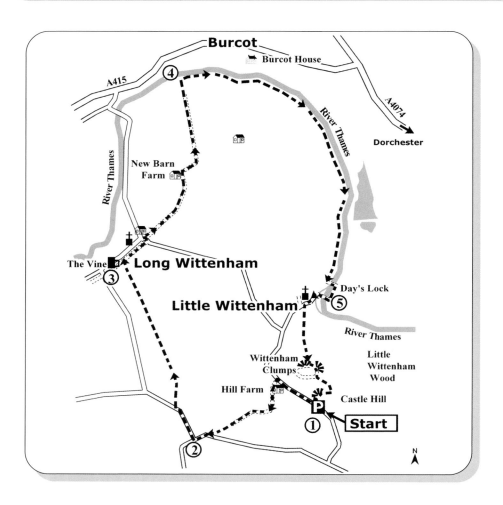

Introduction

This is an easy walk to the attractive village of Long Wittenham and along the bank of the River Thames, leaving it at Day's Lock to arrive in the hamlet of Little Wittenham and to enter the Nature Reserve (managed by the Northmoor Trust who established it in 1982). A short ascent takes you to Wittenham Clumps (known locally as 'The Clumps') for the outstanding Thames Valley view over the Cotswolds, Chilterns and the Ridgeway. Perhaps stroll into the woodland below the hill, where you may be lucky enough to see a muntjac deer, or maybe a heron or a kingfisher near the ponds, before returning to your car.

The Vine Inn

You are guaranteed a warm welcome at the partly-thatched 16th-century Vine Inn in Long Wittenham. There is a superb bar menu and lasagne, chilli, curry, steak and veggie dishes (Old Oxford sausage, mash and gravy is something special) can all be finished off with one of the great puds on offer. Alternatively, you can select from the specials board. Good home-cooked food is the order of the day with food available during the week from 12 noon to 2.30 pm and from 7 pm to 10 pm (10.30 pm on Saturday). On Sunday you can enjoy a Sunday roast between 12 noon and 4 pm. The real ales of Morland Original and IPA are on tap, together with guest beers. Children and dogs are welcome in the large garden. Telephone: 01865 407832.

THE WALK

(1)

From the car park, stroll down the road in a north-westerly direction. In about 375 yards, immediately after passing **Hill Farm**, turn left past the farm buildings. Continue up a green farm track into open countryside. Initially the track aims south and then it arcs right. You walk to the left of the field hedge and then switch to the right as you near a road. A stile leads onto the road and you head right along its edge towards **Long Wittenham.**

 (2)

At the road corner (GR 555920), bear right and then, just after the next road bend, go right over a stile and walk the clear footpath set to the left of the field hedge to arrive in the village of **Long Wittenham** at a track. Turn right – the **Vine Inn** is on the left and you may enter through the rear garden to visit it at this point.

  (3)

Return to the track and head left, passing along the backs of houses. You will soon pass the **Machine Man**, a former pub that has become bed and breakfast accommodation, to reach a lane. Turn left and then go right onto a tarmac path, passing a converted thatched property. Soon the tarmac gives way to grass and you walk a wide hedged track until you reach the **River Thames**.

 (4)

At the river, turn right onto the **Thames Path**, passing **Burcot House** and the **Chester Homes** premises on the opposite bank. You may see grebe, herons, ducks, moorhens, coots and Canada geese, while boats large and small will pass you by as you progress along the path, going through a series of bridlegates before you reach **Day's Lock**. Cross over the **Thames** and pause to watch the boats making their way through the lock gates. When you are ready, leave

Drive and Stroll

Day's Lock at Little Wittenham

the lock via the hand-gate and turn right, walking up to **Little Wittenham Bridge**.

  (5)

Cross over the bridge and continue over a second bridge, strolling up the lane to see the beautiful 14th-century **St Peter's church** in **Little Wittenham**. From the church proceed through the hand-gate opposite and ascend the clear footpath to the top of **Wittenham Clumps** to enjoy the superb view. Continue by going left around the **Clumps** and then ascend the

steps onto **Castle Hill** and proceed into the trees.

In the midst of the trees on Castle Hill is the Poem Tree, on which Joseph Tubb carved a poem in 1844–45. Thirty different varieties of butterflies and 120 species of birds have been counted in the reserve.

At the path junction, go right and a well-used footpath will lead you back into the open, where you arc left to reach the road by your parked car.

PLACES OF INTEREST NEARBY

Dorchester-on-Thames is only a mile away across the fields. It is a charming, picturesque village set amidst water meadows, with a wonderful abbey in beautiful gardens, and one of the largest churches in Oxfordshire. Website: www.dorchester-on-thames.co.uk

16 | Wallingford

The bridge at Wallingford over the River Thames

The Walk 4 miles
Terrain A level walk along good paths
Map OS Explorer 170 Abingdon, Wantage and Vale of the White Horse
(GR 611894)

How to get there

From the north approach Wallingford on the A4074. Turn right at the Crowmarsh Gifford road junction into Wallingford. **Parking:** In the municipal pay and display car park on the right near the swimming pool, just before reaching Wallingford bridge.

Drive and Stroll

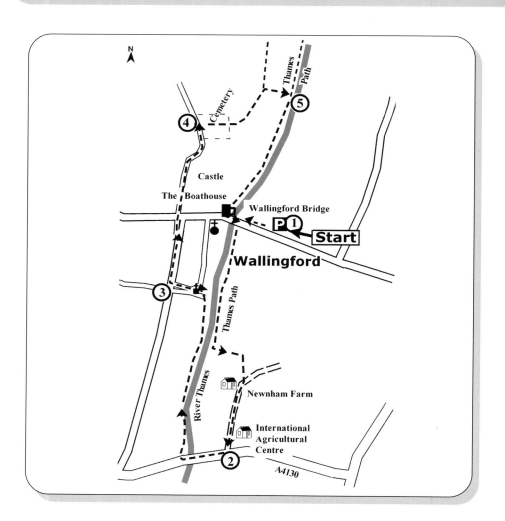

Introduction

This pleasant walk offers the chance to explore historic Wallingford. The town was founded by King Alfred in the 10th century and still has some impressive earthworks and fortifications. From the banks of the River Thames there are fine views of the lovely Wallingford Bridge, and after passing through the town you will have the opportunity to visit the Norman castle remains and then stroll again along the Thames Path, to arrive near to the Boathouse for refreshments before returning over Wallingford Bridge to your car.

The Boathouse

There can be few finer pleasures than supping a pint on the banks of the River Thames, watching the boating world go by. The Boathouse is sited in an idyllic spot next to the historic bridge, with outstanding views over the longest lock-free stretch of the famous river. It is open all day every day between 12 noon and 11 pm, and a wide selection of real ales and Strongbow cider is available. Food is available between 12 noon and 8 pm when one can choose from the traditional menu of light snacks or go for a hearty meal.

There is a superb garden/patio overlooking the river and children are allowed in the bar and the garden. Dogs are restricted to the garden/patio and must be kept on their lead and under control at all times. Telephone: 01491 834100.

THE WALK

(1)

From the car park, stroll down to the bank of the **River Thames**, passing beneath **Wallingford Bridge** onto the **Thames Path**. You walk south along this for about ½ mile. You will enjoy a pleasing view of the beautiful bridge, with the fine steeple of **St Peter's church** adding to the scene. After passing through a second gateway, you will see **Newnham Farm** ahead of you. Turn left and pass to the left of the farm buildings onto a farm track. Walk this track between the buildings, maintaining a southerly direction and continue ahead along a hedged path, passing the buildings of the **International Agricultural Information Centre** (on your left) until you arrive at the A4130.

 (2)

Turn right along the pavement over the **Thames** and then turn right again, descending to the **Thames**

Path once more, now on the west bank of the river. Walk along the clear path and go over the footbridge across **Bradford Brook**.

Note the Thames Conservancy building which displays flood marks indicating the water levels of 1897, 1947 and 1979. You walk at the back of some attractive houses that all have their own landing stage, and you will notice that a number of these have a wide concrete area to the left of the footpath – many years ago this was all part of an airstrip for light aircraft.

Continue along the hedge-lined path to arrive at a lane that arcs left. At the lane corner, turn right through a passageway under a house and proceed over a stream, noting the lovely black and white building to the left. Continue up the path by **St Leonard's church** to arrive at the front of the church in **St Leonard's Lane**. Take time to stroll around the churchyard, which is a conservation

Drive and Stroll

The Boathouse seen from Wallingford Bridge

area and has a number of interesting plants, with labels of identification. Continue up **St Leonard's Lane** until you reach **St Mary's Street**.

 ③

Turn right along **St Mary's Street**, passing the market square where you can visit **St Mary Le More church** – the **Tourist Information Office** is sited in the town hall. Note the sign that records the 800th anniversary of the town (1155 to 1955) and the stork memorial. Continue along **St Mary's Street** until you reach **High Street**. Cross over **High Street** with care and proceed up **Castle Street**

opposite, taking the opportunity to visit **Castle Gardens** and to explore what is left of the Norman castle.

By 1066, Wallingford housed the Royal Mint and was the leading town in Berkshire. After victory at Hastings, William the Conqueror arrived and ordered a royal castle to be built and among its many occupants were King John, Edward the Black Prince and Henry VI. Later, in 1155, Henry II granted a Charter permitting a Guild and Burgesses to hold regular markets. During the Civil War, the castle came under siege by Oliver Cromwell but after a long twelve weeks the defenders were forced to surrender and Cromwell ordered its demolition in 1652. Sadly, only the earthworks remain.

Continue along the pavement of **Castle Street**, walking out of **Wallingford**.

When you reach the cemetery, turn right onto a signed track that passes through the cemetery grounds. It soon arcs left, then bends right to arrive back on the **Thames Path**.

Turn right and stroll along the path towards **Wallingford**. After about ½ mile the castle will be to your right and then you pass between buildings to arrive in **Castle Lane**. Pass to the right of the **Boathouse pub** to reach the **High Street**. Turn left over **Wallingford Bridge** and return to the parking area.

PLACES OF INTEREST NEARBY

Nuffield Place, 9 miles east, is the former home of William Morris, later Lord Nuffield, founder of Morris Motors. It is a superb example of a 1930s upper middle-class home and many of the rooms are still decorated in the fashion of that age. Classic and veteran cars are often on display in the grounds. Telephone: 01491 641224 for details of open days.

In the nearby village of **Nettlebed**, there is a 300-year-old kiln which was used to make the bricks for Wallingford Castle.

17 White Horse Wander

Dragon Hill

The Walk 5½ miles
Terrain Generally easy walking, with some undulations
Map OS Explorer 170 Abingdon, Wantage and Vale of the White Horse
(GR 294866)

How to get there

Whitehorse Hill is to the west of Wantage on the B4507. Turn south at the crossroads opposite the turning to Woolstone. **Parking:** In the National Trust free car park.

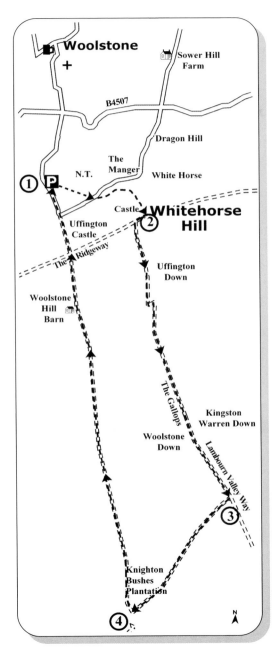

Introduction

No guide to Oxfordshire would be complete without a walk around the wonderful White Horse at Uffington. Take your camera on this exceptional walk, for there are many photo opportunities and superb views. Measuring 360 ft by 126 ft, the White Horse is an impressive sight and is believed to be Britain's oldest and most famous hill figure – some 2,000 to 3,000 years old. There are numerous theories as to its origin, but historians believe it is Iron Age or Anglo-Saxon. The monument became very overgrown in the 19th century but it has been restored and is now cared for by the National Trust. The route then joins part of the Lambourn Valley Way for a very fine stretch of hill walking and more wonderful views all around.

The White Horse

The White Horse inn at Woolstone, built around 1540, is a chocolate-box building. By the time you reach the inn you will be ready for one of its cask range of beers – Akle and Hook Norton are among the real ales on offer while Scrumpy Jack and Blackthorn Dry will please the cider drinkers. From Monday to Saturday, the freehouse inn opens between 11 am (12 noon on Sunday) and 3 pm, and 6 pm to 11 pm (7 pm to 10.30 pm on Sunday). Food is available between 11 am (12 noon on Sunday) and 3 pm, and from 6 pm to 10 pm (7 pm to 10.30 pm on Sunday). A full bar menu as well as an à la carte menu offers a wide selection of truly appetising foods and it is a delight to eat out in the attractive garden on a sunny day. You can be assured of a warm welcome and accommodation is available if you wish to stay in the area to complete more of the local walks. Children are allowed in the inn but dogs are not permitted. Telephone: 01367 820726.

THE WALK

Leave the rear of the car park onto the hillside and walk the clear footpath towards **Whitehorse Hill**. A hand-gate allows you to cross the road and you then ascend to the top of the hill – to your left is the famous **White Horse**. Proceed up to the trig point (259m) for a truly magnificent view over the vale, stretching as far as the **Cotswolds**.

The Manger is a spectacular dry valley with ripples (Giant Steps) formed by the effect of snow melting at the end of the last Ice Age. Dragon Hill is the strange, flat hilltop below the White Horse and this is where legend says that St George slew the dragon – the dragon's blood was so poisoned that the grass never grew, leaving the white patches you see today. Uffington Castle was originally constructed in the late Bronze Age, probably in the 7th or 8th century BC; it then consisted of ramparts with massive timber gates and an associated linear ditch.

Leave the **National Trust** area via a kissing-gate to arrive on the **Ridgeway**.

Turn right and walk along the famous track for just 300 yards, then turn left down a clear, wide track set to the left of the fence. This lovely path zigzags left and then right for you to continue along a good fenced path – the **Lambourn Valley Way**. The path ascends to the left of trees and then you arrive in wide, open countryside. Follow the signed route, walking between some white posts as you proceed southwards. You are walking part of the **Gallops** and should look out for horses being exercised. Soon, to your left, you will see **Idlebush Barrow**. Continue down the wide green track and take in the superb views all around. To the left is **Kingston Warren Down** and you can enjoy this easy walking for a further ½ mile before reaching a junction of tracks.

Turn right and continue the gentle descent along a wide bridleway set to the left of the fence – ahead is a

The White Horse at Woolstone

lovely valley view as you descend towards the trees of **Knighton Bushes Plantation**. The track arcs to the left of the plantation and soon you arrive at another junction of tracks.

 (4)

Turn right and walk up the track for the next 2 miles. This takes you to the left of **Knighton Bushes Plantation**, and in about 500 yards you pass through a strip of beech trees. A further mile takes you past **Woolstone Hill Barn** and then you soon arrive back on the **Ridgeway**. Cross over and continue up the track opposite. This becomes a tarmac road in about 400 yards. Continue ahead to return to the car park.

PLACES OF INTEREST NEARBY

Wayland's Smithy is a mile west of the White Horse along the Ridgeway (GR 281858). It is a prehistoric site associated with Wayland, the Norse god of blacksmiths, and is at least 1,000 years older than Stonehenge – the long burial chamber measures 185 ft long by 43 ft wide and is set in a sheltering grove of beech trees. Website: www.mysteriousbritain.co.uk

18 Letcombe Regis

The former watercress beds at Letcombe Brook

The Walk 4½ miles
Terrain A small hill ascent leads to good tracks and undulating footpaths
Map OS Explorer 170 Abingdon, Wantage and Vale of the White Horse (GR 374849)

How to get there

From the B4507, about 2½ miles west of Wantage, turn south onto the B4001 and follow the signs into Letcombe Bassett. **Parking:** With consideration along the roadside in Letcombe Bassett; the walk begins by the church.

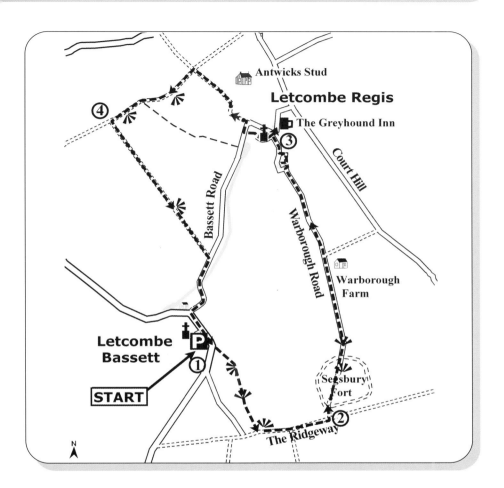

Introduction

This delightful walk offers the opportunity to visit an area of the county famed for its horseracing achievements. It starts from the small, friendly 12th-century church in the beautiful village of Letcombe Bassett, where timber-framed, thatched cottages abound. The walk then continues into attractive countryside to join the Ridgeway before crossing Segsbury Fort to arrive in Letcombe Regis. After passing through the historic village and by Antwicks Stud, you ascend onto a lovely track and then descend to cross over Letcombe Brook near the once-famous Letcombe Bassett watercress beds, where you may see racehorses drinking, before returning back into the village.

Drive and Stroll

The Greyhound Inn

This impressive Grade II listed building in Letcombe Regis was built in the 17th century and it was on its very doorstep in the early 1900s that the Riot Act was supposedly read for the last time in England. The Greyhound is noted for its early 19th-century brickwork, which uses a Flemish bond with black glazed headers. Letcombe Regis is famous in the racing world as the training base of no fewer than three Grand National winners and therefore the name of the 'Greyhound' seems rather odd! Monday to Thursday the pub is open from noon to 2.30 pm and from 5.30 pm to 11 pm, but it is open all day from Friday to Sunday. This is a cosy place where you can relax with a pint of Morlands Original, Greene King, Wells Bombardier or perhaps a Blackthorn Cider – they are all in excellent cask condition in the immaculate bar. Food is available from noon to 2 pm and from 6 pm to 9 pm during the week (Sunday evening food finishes at 8.30 pm). The food itself is home-cooked, hearty, wholesome and British, with soups, stews, pies and roasts flying the flag. Lunch can be enjoyed in the attractive, non-smoking, raised dining area or in the garden if you prefer. Telephone: 01235 771093 Email: thegreyhoundinn@supanet.com

THE WALK

The walk begins by the **church of St Michael and All Angels**.

The church is a real gem with Norman scratch dials on the south buttress used to show the hour for Mass. Dean Jonathan Swift is said to have sat under the ancient mulberry tree in the garden of the Old Rectory while writing some of his vitriolic political satires. The tree is more than 300 years old.

From the church, head right up the side of the quiet road ascending **Gramps Hill**. After about 200 yards, at the first bend, turn left onto a waymarked footpath into attractive countryside. After about 175 yards of lovely walking, the path arcs right and descends into a valley, then ascends by the side of woodland. Proceed over a couple of stiles and cross pastureland to arrive at a final stile onto the **Ridgeway**. Turn left and stroll along the famous footpath for about 600 yards.

Now turn left down a broad track over the top of **Segsbury Fort**, an Iron Age fortification, pausing to enjoy the fine view. The track becomes a tarmac lane and this leads along **Warborough Road** into the village of **Letcombe Regis**. At the road bend there is a cottage ahead of you named **The Sparrow** – once one of the two pubs in the village. Pass to the right of **The Sparrow** and bear left

A charming thatched cottage at Letcombe Regis

by **The Anvil** (a beautiful thatched cottage) along a hedged footpath to reach the main road in the village. Turn right to the road junction.

Spare time to stroll up into Letcombe Regis by going right up Main Street – there are some wonderful thatched cottages and the Greyhound Inn. When you are ready, retrace your steps back to the road junction.

  (3)

Proceed ahead over the junction, passing the **church of St Andrew** – the thatched building ahead of you is stunning. When past the church, bear left along a hedged footpath to reach **Bassett Road**. Turn right along

the road to its corner, then head left into open countryside along a well-used, hedged bridlepath ascending out of the valley. To the right you will see the buildings of the **Antwicks Stud**, but you continue up the hill to a junction of tracks. Here, turn left along a green road, enjoying the fine view over **Letcombe Regis** and the surrounding countryside.

  (4)

After walking the track for about ¾ mile, turn left, descend the clear footpath by the field hedge and in about ½ mile you will reach **Bassett Road** once again, Turn right along the road and soon you will cross a delightful bridge over a stream, where

Drive and Stroll

watercress once grew. You are likely to see children playing in and around the water, and horses come here to cool off.

The nearby thatched cottage is the source of the fictitious Arabella's Cottage in Thomas Hardy's novel, Jude the Obscure.

Continue up the road, bearing right to walk through the attractive village of **Letcombe Bassett**. You pass by some superb timbered buildings. The **Yew Tree** is a private house now, but was once the village pub. As you progress up **Gramps Hill**, the church is set back to your right.

PLACES OF INTEREST NEARBY

Didcot Railway Centre, 11 miles to the east, is the home of the Great Western Society and has a unique collection of GWR steam engines, coaches, buildings, etc, as well as a recreation of Brunel's broad gauge railway. Telephone: 01235 817200. Website: www.didcotrailwaycentre.org.uk

You could also plan a visit to **Didcot Power Station** where guided tours are available (booking required in advance). Telephone: 01235 512291. Website: www.npower.com

19 | Stoke Row and the Maharajah's Well

The Maharaja's Well at Stoke Row

The Walk 4½ miles
Terrain A level walk on good footpaths and farm tracks
Map OS Explorer 171 Chiltern Hills West

How to get there

Stoke Row is situated south of the A4130 between Henley-on-Thames and Wallingford. Turn south on the B481 towards Sonning Common and in 2 miles turn right to Stoke Row. The Cherry Tree Inn is on the right. **Parking:** In the Cherry Tree Inn car park, with the landlord's permission.

Drive and Stroll

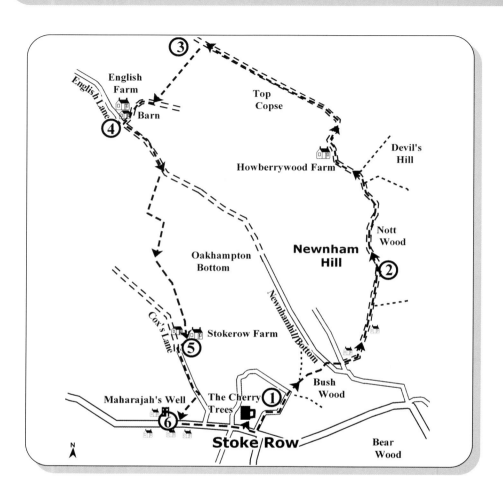

Introduction

Stoke Row is situated within an area of outstanding beauty within the Chilterns – a place of picturesque villages and delightful countryside where the Ridgeway and Thames Path National Trails provide numerous leisure opportunities. This easy walk starts from the Cherry Tree Inn and takes you on good tracks and through superb beech woodland to experience this lovely countryside at its best. You arrive back in the village near to the famous well, given to Stoke Row by the Maharajah of Benares, which is 368 ft deep (more than twice the height of Nelson's Column in London) with a highly ornate wellhead cover – there is a golden elephant under the oriental domed canopy.

The Cherry Tree Inn

The Cherry Tree Inn is a 400-year-old listed building offering a warm welcome and good food. It has a period lounge with timber ceilings and attractive gardens for those sunny days. It is open every day from 12 noon to 3 pm and 7 pm to 10 pm. At weekends food can be enjoyed from 12 noon to 4 pm and 7 pm to 10 pm. The inn offers a choice of classic European dishes served with a modern twist from roast cod on a pea and mint purée, with an oyster and chive cream sauce, to confit of duck leg salad with baby spinach, smoked black pudding and pine kernels. Telephone: 01491 680430. Website: www.thecherrytreeinn.com

THE WALK

From the car park of the **Cherry Tree Inn**, turn left. In 100 yards turn left up the road signed to '**Sports Ground & Pavilion**'. After passing a church building the road bends first right and then left, and at the next corner **Bush Wood** is ahead. Enter the woodland, walking ahead along the clear footpath into the trees. At the junction of footpaths bear right, descending through the trees. After 300 yards of delightful gentle descent, you reach and cross over a lane, then ascend the bank opposite crossing a second lane. Proceed up a very quiet lane past several houses and in about ½ mile you will reach a house on the edge of **Nott Wood**.

Pass to the left of the house and enter the wood on a clear bridlepath, passing through mainly beech trees. Bear right at the track junction and the track soon bends left exiting the trees, with **Howberrywood Farm** ahead. Pass between the farm buildings and bear right. Soon the track bends left and you will be walking a hedged farm track with trees to your left. At the end of the trees there is an opening and you will see **English Farm** across the valley to your left.

Go left over the field stile and walk the clear, well-used footpath, generally aiming towards the farmhouse. Leave the field via the farm gate set to the left of fencing, to arrive on a farm track. Now turn right to stroll up the good track towards the farmhouse. You pass a superb barn and the front of the lovely farmhouse to arrive on a track called **English Lane**.

Turn left along the track for about 500 yards, then go right over a stile, ascending to the left of a field fence and pausing near the top of the rise for a pleasing retrospective view. At the field end, go over the stile and head left along a narrow hedged footpath. In 100 yards, go right over a stile and cross pastureland to enter

Drive and Stroll

The bridleway through Nott...

woodland via a further stile. Stroll down the clear footpath inside the wood and exit at its bottom. Continue up the side of the field hedge and at the top of the field veer left through a farm gate. Then bear right up a driveway towards **Stokerow Farm**, passing through a couple of farm gates. Pass the farmhouse, then turn right up the main drive to a track called **Cox's Lane**.

 (5)

Turn left along **Cox's Lane** towards **Stoke Row**. In 350 yards, turn right (just after passing the entrance driveway to **Pond House**) and stroll up a hedged footpath into the village.

At the main road in the village you will find the impressive **Maharajah's Well** to the right.

Stoke Row was once an important centre for the brickmaking industry and for very many years had a water supply problem. This was largely solved in 1863 when the Maharajah of Benares provided the village with a well to show his appreciation for help given to him in India by Edward Anderson Reade of nearby Ipsden.

(6)

Head left through the village to return to the **Cherry Tree Inn**, where refreshment awaits.

PLACES OF INTEREST NEARBY

Ewelme, 7 miles to the north-west, is a delightful village full of history. You must visit the very beautiful Duchess's Almshouses, and spare time in the churchyard to find the stone that reads: 'For we are labourers together with God' – here lies Jerome K. Jerome, one of the early laughtermakers. The inside walls of the chapel of St George are covered in medieval blackletter caligraphy. Website: www.ewelme.info

20 | Whitchurch-on-Thames

A fine view from Hadstock Nature Reserve

The Walk 6 miles
Terrain An easy walk on good paths, with just one small hill to ascend
Map OS Explorer 171 Chiltern Hills West

How to get there

From Pangbourne on the A329, turn north on the B471 to pass through Whitchurch-on-Thames. **Parking:** By the war memorial north of Whitchurch-on-Thames, on the B471.

Drive and Stroll

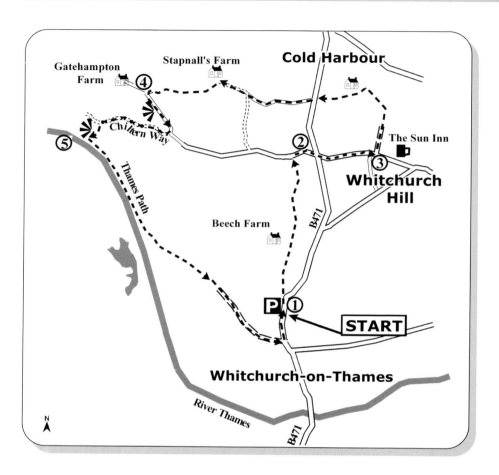

Introduction

This is red kite country and you should look out for these lovely birds soaring high in the skies on this easy walk. It starts from the war memorial at the picturesque village of Whitchurch-on-Thames. The River Thames, which runs through the village, provides a tranquil background with beautiful water meadows. On the other side of the Thames is Pangbourne, which is connected to Whitchurch via a toll bridge. The walk continues across undulating open countryside onto Whitchurch Hill and leads you into the quiet village of Hill Bottom, where you can rest for refreshments. More lovely woodland paths and part of the Chiltern Way lead to a fine view over the River Thames and you walk part of the Thames Path on the way back to the war memorial.

The Sun Inn

When you visit the Sun Inn at Hill Bottom you are assured of fine ale, good food and a hearty welcome. It is very much a family pub where children and dogs (under strict control) are made welcome. A good range of real ales is available including Brakspear and Hooray Henry, along with Strongbow cider. It is a pleasure to sit out in the garden on a sunny day in the summer and sup a pint. The inn is open every day of the week and the Sunday roast is a real plateful which will test the hungry walker. Reasonably priced good food is available between noon and 3 pm during the day and from 7 pm to 9 pm in the evenings. The Woodland Fruit Strudel is rather special. Telephone: 0118 9842260.

THE WALK

From the **war memorial**, head up the left-hand side of the B471 for about 100 yards, then bear left to a kissing-gate into farm fields. Now walk along the path set to the right of the field hedge over a couple of fields. Pass through a kissing-gate and continue past **Beech Farm**, following the waymarked route through hand-gates and into the trees. Bear right through the next hand-gate onto a fenced footpath going towards the gamekeeper's cottage and you will reach a wide track that leads onto a lane. Turn right down the lane for 160 yards to arrive at the B471.

Cross over the B471 and walk the pavement of the road opposite into **Hill Bottom**. Soon you will see **Box Cottage** on the left.

The Sun Inn is up the road ahead, if you wish to stop for refreshments.

Immediately before reaching **Box Cottage**, turn left up **Cashes Lane** and ascend into the woodland called **Great Oaks**. The clear footpath arcs left inside the trees and in about 250 yards you reach a junction of paths. Bear left and exit the trees, walking along a footpath that arcs westwards through a field of wildflowers, with the buildings of **Great Oaks School** over the hedge to your right. You will pass through more woodland and soon arrive at the B471 once again.

Cross over the road and continue along the lane opposite. It enters trees, where bluebells add colour in the spring. When you reach a track junction, bear left. This track soon arcs right and joins the lane that leads towards **Stapnall's Farm**, now stables. Just before reaching the driveway to **Chalkward Cottage**, turn left through a white gate. Cross over a field, where there may be horses, then go through a hand-gate in the far right-hand corner to stroll along a

Drive and Stroll

The working watermill at Mapledurham is worth visiting

clear footpath through the delightful trees of **Great Chalk Wood** – in spring you will be walking amid the bluebells. Initially you pass through the middle of the woodland and then along its left-hand edge to arrive in the open.

At the end of the driveway to **Gatehampton Farm**, bear left (south-east) along a fenced track/tarmac lane and enjoy a pleasing view to your right. At the trees it arcs right and then bends left. Now, turn right and descend the signed **Chiltern Way path**, walking a hedged gully going west. After about ½ mile you reach a junction of paths and a track. Turn left through a kissing-gate into a nature reserve and ascend a hillock for a fine view. As you descend the other side of the hillock, go over a stile into the woodland of **Hadstock Nature Reserve**, then descend to the **Thames Path** (a National Trail).

Turn left along the **Thames Path** – you will have glimpses of the river to your right through the trees. After walking the path for about ¾ mile, it arcs gently left away from the river to arrive in open countryside on a hedged footpath, which leads onto a farm track/lane. Walk along this quiet lane as it arcs gently, passing several farms and a horse training centre. Eventually you arrive at the B471 on the outskirts of **Whitchurch-on-Thames**. Cross over the B471 and head left up the raised footpath on the other side of the road. In 550 yards, cross back over the road to the car park by the war memorial.

PLACES OF INTEREST NEARBY

Mapledurham, 4 miles south-east, nestles on the banks of the Thames and is the historic home of the Blount family. There is a superb working watermill to visit. Telephone: 01189 723350; www.mapledurham.co.uk

Other walking titles by Countryside Books
covering the county include:

PUB STROLLS IN OXFORDSHIRE
Roger Noyce

ADVENTUROUS PUB WALKS IN OXFORDSHIRE
Roger Noyce

PUB WALKS FOR MOTORISTS:
BERKSHIRE & OXFORDSHIRE
Lee Maple

PUB WALKS ALONG THE RIDGEWAY
Charles Whynne-Hammond

THAMES VALLEY ILLUSTRATED WALKS
Trevor Yorke

POCKET PUB WALKS IN THE THAMES VALLEY
Nick Channer